Entrepreneur
MAGAZINE'S

start*up*

Start Your Own

2ND EDITION

CAR WASH AND MORE

Full-Service ♦ *In-Bay Automatic*
Exterior Conveyor ♦ *Self-Service*

Entrepreneur Press and Rich Mintzer

EP
Entrepreneur
Press

Additional titles in *Entrepreneur's* **Startup Series**

Start Your Own

Bed & Breakfast

Business on eBay

Business Support Service

Child Care Service

Cleaning Service

Clothing Store

Coin-Operated Laundry

Consulting

Crafts Business

e-Business

e-Learning Business

Event Planning Business

Executive Recruiting Service

Freight Brokerage Business

Gift Basket Service

Growing and Selling Herbs
 and Herbal Products

Home Inspection Service

Import/Export Business

Information Consultant Business

Law Practice

Lawn Care Business

Mail Order Business

Medical Claims Billing Service

Personal Concierge Service

Personal Training Business

Pet-Sitting Business

Restaurant and Five Other
 Food Businesses

Self-Publishing Business

Seminar Production Business

Specialty Travel & Tour Business

Staffing Service

Successful Retail Business

Vending Business

Wedding Consultant Business

Wholesale Distribution Business

Start Your Own

CAR WASH
AND MORE

Editorial Director: Jere L. Calmes
Managing Editor: Marla Markman
Cover Design: Beth Hansen-Winter
Production and Composition: studio Salt

This publication is designed to provide accurate and authoritative information in regard to the subject matter covered. It is sold with the understanding that the publisher is not engaged in rendering legal, accounting, or other professional services. If legal advice or other expert assistance is required, the services of a competent professional person should be sought.

Library of Congress Cataloging-in-Publication Data is available
Mintzer, Richard.
    Start your own car wash and more/Entrepreneur Press and Rich Mintzer.—2nd ed.
      p.   cm.
    Rev. ed. of: Start your own car wash / Chris Simeral. c2003.
    ISBN-13: 978-1-59918-101-1 (alk. paper)
    ISBN-10: 1-59918-101-0 (alk. paper)
      1. Car wash industry—Management. 2. New business enterprises—Management.
3. Entrepreneurship. I. Simeral, Chris. Start your own car wash. II. Entrepreneur Press.
III. Title.
HD9999.C272S54 2007
629.28'7—dc22   2007005928

Printed in Canada

11 10 09 08 07   10 9 8 7 6 5 4 3 2 1

83609983

Contents

▲

▲

Chapter 9
Income and Expenses

Chapter 10
Advertising, Marketing, and Public Relations

▲

Preface

For as long as cars are around, their owners will need car washes. That's what makes car washes one of the more attractive start-ups out there. You can start as big or as small as you want, constrained only by the amount of start-up capital you can get your hands on and the time you're willing to spend to make the business a success. You can operate a small, self-serve operation in your spare time, or go all out with a complete full-service shop with a dozen employees or more. Either way, you'll undoubtedly face some challenges along the way, and that's what this guide is for.

In this book, you'll discover what a car wash is, and, perhaps more importantly, what it is not. Going into any business venture with your eyes open is vital to its eventual success, especially if you truly plan to make a go of it. It is important that you keep your eyes open to the possibilities, and the drawbacks, with any location you examine for a new wash—and especially if you are dealing with the seller of an existing business who claims, whether honestly or not, to be "practically giving the business away." A car wash can be a very profitable business to be sure. However, no matter how long the line outside the car wash, you need to remember that if it is not run well and promoted on a steady basis, a car wash is not guaranteed to succeed.

Finally, if there's one thing I discovered over the course of writing this book, it is that many people currently in the car wash business don't necessarily feel like talking about how they succeeded. The reason is simple—competition. No one wants a competing business right across the street, especially if that competitor is privy to how you made your business work. But with that being said, there were some owners generous enough to share their time and expertise with me. I'd like to thank them for giving me many of the tips, tricks, and tactics for building a successful car wash business. You'll find some of their words of wisdom within this book.

Why Start a Car Wash Business?

You've probably never stopped to think about where your local car wash fits into the grand scheme of the car wash industry. The only thing you know is that when your car gets dirty you need to wash it, and the closest place to get that done is probably where you go.

Maybe you've spent some time considering opening a car wash business of your own while waiting in line for a wash on a bright and sunny Saturday morning. You've probably seen a dozen or more cars in queue, with each owner paying between $5 and $15 for a wash that they may not even find totally satisfactory. If you're like many entrepreneurs, you may have started doing some quick math in your head—projecting what the car wash owner is probably making in one month, then one year. Maybe you even thought, "Boy, this place is a cash cow!"

Finally it's your turn. As you watch your car move through the tunnel, you see how automated the process is, how quickly it gets done, how little actual work seems to be required. "How hard could this possibly be? Anyone can make money running a car wash!" you might have thought.

Most car wash owners can share a wink and a smile at the naïveté of the average neophyte. Many people think a car wash is a great business opportunity because they see it as a business that doesn't require a great deal of hands-on work but still produces a great return on your investment. The reality is a bit more complicated than that. It's not exactly a mystery, but ask any car wash owner, and he will tell you the same thing—"It's not as easy as it looks."

What a Car Wash Is and Isn't

When most people think of a car wash, they tend to think of an exterior-conveyor wash. These are the washes that put cars on a motorized track and drag them through a tunnel where they are rinsed, soaped up, washed, rinsed again, and possibly waxed.

The cars then emerge clean (and perhaps even relatively dry) at the other end. But this is only one type of car wash. Other types of washes include the following:

Stat Fact
According to the president of the International Carwash Association, there are approximately 75,000 car washes in the United States.

- *Full-service.* This is basically a combination of the exterior conveyor with an additional inside cleaning.
- *In-bay automatic (also called a rollover).* This type of car wash is an automatic wash consisting of a machine that literally "rolls over" a stationary car parked in a washing bay.
- *Self-service.* Most self-service car washes are coin- or token-operated brush-and-hose combinations that the driver uses to dispense soap, wash the car, and rinse it off.

We'll discuss in more detail what's involved with each of these types of washes in a minute. But for now, let's stick with the mental picture of the exterior-conveyor car wash, as we learn more about the ins and outs of this business. The best place to start is by examining a few common misconceptions most people have about what a typical car wash business involves.

Myth #1: This Business Is a Cash Cow

Sure, if you drive by your local car wash on a sunny Saturday morning, you'll see cars waiting in line for a wash. But drive by that same car wash on a rainy Thursday afternoon, and you'll be lucky if you see one or two cars waiting. You might even see that the shop is closed for the day. Variables such as the time of the week as well as the weather will affect the profitability of a car wash. Additionally, people are sometimes content to let their cars stay dirty for "one more day."

Myth #2: This Is a Hands-Off Business

As an outsider, all you see are cars being dragged along a conveyor as a bunch of gizmos and doodads spray, buff, rinse, wax, and even dry them. You might not ever see a human being doing any work at all. In truth though, this is not a business that you can put on autopilot. For one thing, those gizmos and doodads can and will break down. And, depending on the type of equipment you buy, they might break down much more than you think.

Cars will also emerge from those washing tunnels and not be clean enough to satisfy some customers. They may also have a scratch that you didn't cause but that the customer blames you for anyway. Employees sometimes will not treat customers the way they should be treated, especially if you haven't trained them well. Shipments of supplies will be late or you may be billed incorrectly. Making sure you have enough supplies on hand is imperative. After all, it's pretty much impossible to wash a car with no soap. The bottom line is that you'll be spending a lot of time at your car wash—at least until you learn the business well enough to be able to hire a professional manager who can take over when you're not there.

Myth #3: You Won't Have Employees to Worry About

This might actually be true for certain types of car washes (most likely self-service and, to a lesser extent, in-bay automatic washes), but for a full-service or exterior-conveyor wash, you're going to have to hire employees and inherit the headaches and responsibilities that go along with them. In fact, aside from the initial investment in equipment and commercial space, employees will probably be one of the biggest costs you incur while running your business.

Myth #4: You're in Total Control

Well, you are your own boss, that's for sure. But until someone figures out how to control factors such as the weather, you're still going to have to answer to a higher authority. No matter how much time you put into your business, there are still going to be things that go wrong—things you just cannot control.

Even if you're a mechanical whiz, some of your equipment is going to break down. And if it happens at a peak washing time, like that glorious sunny Saturday morning we keep talking about, you're going to watch a lot of potential profit go down the drain.

You will have to suffer through days, or maybe even weeks at a time (depending on where your business is located), when the weather is so bad that the farthest thing from anyone's mind is getting a car wash. And unfortunately, the bank won't care about the lousy weather when your loan payment comes due.

Now for the Good News

By now, you're probably having one of two reactions. You're either (a) sorry that you bought this book because what you've just learned is sapping your enthusiasm for opening a business that you thought would be a breeze, or, (b) you're thankful that you bought this book because you think it may have saved you from wasting your money opening a business that you thought would be a breeze.

But before you start looking elsewhere for that great business opportunity, consider this: Many people have made a lot of money washing cars. It's a service that is always in demand and that most consumers are certainly willing to pay for.

The point in telling you about the pitfalls first is to make you think clearly and critically about just what it is you're getting into when you open a car wash. Yes, there is the opportunity to make lots of money and have fun doing it—but only if you put in the work required to make your business a success. The rest of this book will deal with how to do just that. Let's get started by examining the origins of the industry, where it is right now, and where it might be headed in the near future.

Past, Present, and Future

Imagine sitting around a room and listening to a bunch of car wash vets waxing poetic about the good old days of the industry. If you eavesdropped on their conversation, you might hear them talking about the days when customers would come in for a full-service wash and think nothing of waiting an hour or more for the job to be completed. Or maybe they might talk about not having to compete with the latest dotcom start-up or fast-food chain for motivated employees. But whatever the specific topic of conversation, chances are it would center around one thing—how the industry has changed, and how they've had to adapt in order to build and grow their businesses.

Thinking Regionally

As the 21st century began, there was a movement by some large companies to try to consolidate the car wash business. As Kate Carr, editor of *Professional Carwashing & Detailing* magazine, explains, "Everybody wanted to start up a national car wash and brand it like a MacDonald's. It's not as easy because of labor issues and differences in regions of the country, so a lot of them closed down. Even Wash Depot, the largest chain in the country, with about 70 places, went through a tough time before they made a go of it." For the most part, Carr and others in the industry have seen that cross-country consolidation has not caught on. "Most car washes are individually owned, or perhaps an owner will have three or four washes regionally. AutoBell is a good example of a successful regional carwash," explains Carr of the popular wash chain in the North Carolina and Virginia region. Still, more than 65 percent of the car wash industry is made up of individually owned washes. Regional expansion has been the only form of consolidation, and even that has only affected certain sections of the country where the geographic area is more homogeneous. In fact, *Professional Carwashing & Detailing* magazine lists the top 50 car wash companies, and all the ones toward the bottom of the list have only around seven washes, meaning there are very few large car wash chains.

The Changing Attitudes of Customers

People today have less and less time to spend on errands such as getting their car washed. One of the main challenges of today's car wash owner isn't just providing customers with clean cars—it's providing customers with clean cars in as short a time as possible. Another challenge is providing the best quality of wash possible.

Express Exterior

One of the latest trends in the industry is the new express exterior wash, where cars move through a 120-foot tunnel on a conveyor belt, with the customer inside. The average price is $5.23 for this type of wash and there are no amenities, no detailing, or interior cleaning. This means very little labor is needed. Some of the facilities have vacuums available where the driver can then pull over after the car has gone through the tunnel and clean the interior for free. This is the latest in "quick" car washes, but how effective they are, and how lucrative they will be, is yet to be determined. FlexServe is another method of car wash, which long-time car wash expert Steve Okun is touting as an alternative to the full-service wash. FlexServe is a method by which operators utilize various options from the full and express camps and are better able to make the necessary changes to accommodate specific situations, such as changes in the weather or in the economic climate. These modern modes of car washing will be discussed again later.

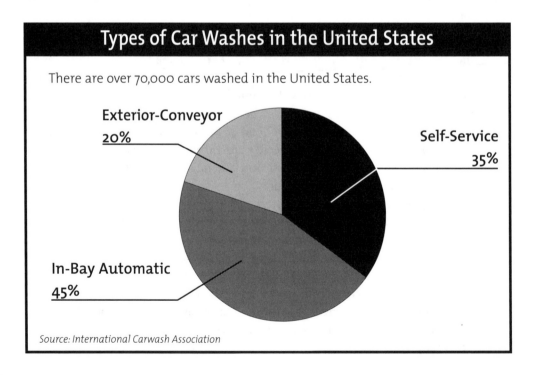

Types of Car Washes in the United States

There are over 70,000 cars washed in the United States.

Exterior-Conveyor 20%

Self-Service 35%

In-Bay Automatic 45%

Source: International Carwash Association

The Blurring of Your Core Business

It used to be that only oil companies offered a car wash with a fill-up. And then, more often than not, the wash would be free. Today, however, many car washes combine the services of a gas station and car wash, or they strike deals with neighboring filling stations for car wash discounts.

In the past, a customer would be lucky to get a free cup of coffee while waiting for his car to be washed. Today, the average car wash customer is likely to find a wide array of snack foods at his disposal in the car wash "gift shop." Some owners even sell greeting cards and pocketbooks alongside the more traditional air fresheners and key chains in their gift shop. While some veterans in the business will argue that this is blurring the main objective – washing cars – others will argue that more profit centers mean more profits, especially on slow or rainy days.

According to Kate Carr, multiprofit centers, such as convenience stores, are the wave of the future. "Providing coffee, a fast lube job, fast food, or other profit centers that you can fit comfortably onto your property, and manage efficiently, the better off you'll be," says Carr. Other additions include extended detailing services, gold plating, and so on. All of this maximizes potential profit, especially when mild winters cut into the profits of car washes in places like the northeast.

What this points to is a trend toward offering customers multiple services all in one place—a one-stop shopping experience. This only makes sense, since the average customer is more pressed for time than ever before. The more you can combine the services they need, the more likely customers will be to pick your car wash over another.

The Future

Let's face it, if the experts 50 years ago were right, we'd all be flying around in rocket cars by now. While no one can predict the future with accuracy, what we can say is that current trends certainly favor car wash owners. People are buying more-expensive vehicles, and they're keeping them longer and want to maintain them in good condition. And while we may see some dramatic design changes in cars over the coming years—it may soon be the case that we "charge" our cars at home rather than filling them up at the gas station—the business of the car wash owner doesn't seem at risk. No matter what happens, it is likely that as long as there are cars, there will always be a need for car washes.

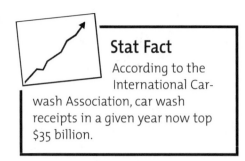

Stat Fact

According to the International Car-wash Association, car wash receipts in a given year now top $35 billion.

With that said, you're about to enter an industry that is undergoing some changes. Some say that the time has never been better for newcomers. Others caution that until the industry "shakes out," committing the time and money required to make a new car wash successful is a risky proposition. Every entrepreneurial endeavor involves risk, and you will have to research your local market diligently and assess your chances for success.

Your Entrepreneurial Spirit

You will also need to evaluate whether a car wash is the right type of business for you. Will you enjoy the tasks that come along with it—fixing machinery, keeping supplies on hand, meeting and dealing with customers, resolving conflicts and crises? Take the self-quiz on page 9 to find out how well-suited you are to working in the car wash industry.

For starters, how energetic are you? If you're someone who falls asleep in front of the TV every night at eight o'clock, you may not be able to put in the time and energy needed to make your business a success. If, on the other hand, you're a dynamo—someone who enjoys expending energy and isn't happy unless you're on the go—you'll have a better chance of being an entrepreneurial success.

How risk-tolerant are you? Risk tolerance refers to your comfort level in relation to the risk associated with starting a new business, or making any kind of investment for that mater. Starting any business involves a certain amount of risk. The question is: Can you tolerate such risks, or will you be staying awake every night pacing the floor each time you have a slow day? Once you start your own business, you will no longer be getting a steady paycheck, and it's likely that your income will vary widely from week to week and month to month. This isn't only true when you're starting a business—it will probably continue for months or even years. You're going to have your slow months, and you're going to have your hot months. This can be especially true with a car wash business because of various factors, some of which (like the weather) will be out of your control. How well can you handle the ebb and flow? If you can absorb the hits you're going to take when money is slow to come in, you'll be able to stick around and enjoy it when business picks up again. In short, you shouldn't be someone who wants to throw in the towel at the first sign of trouble.

How self-motivated are you? Are you someone who stops trying to improve something when you feel that it's "good enough"? To be sure, there's something to be said for leaving well enough alone. But unless you're constantly striving to take steps to make your business even better, you run the risk of having your business become stale or obsolete. No one would want the economy as a whole to just remain where it is right now and not grow, and it's the same thing with your car wash. If you make $100,000 in your first year, are you the kind of person who's going to push yourself to make $125,000 the next? Do you need someone to give you the motivation to do that, or can you find the motivation within yourself? After all, if you aren't concerned about growing your business, who will be?

You also need to be ready and willing to grow with the industry. For example, technology changes quickly. By the time you finish reading this book, some new time-saving or energy-saving device has probably hit the market. Okay, maybe it's not that fast, but you can be sure that new equipment, chemicals, and products for a more efficient, modernized car wash are being worked on constantly by manufacturers. Therefore,

Personality Traits and Preferences Self-Quiz

Are you the type of person who should own a car wash? All of the personality traits or preferences listed below would be helpful to a new car wash owner. While there's no score that either qualifies or disqualifies you for car wash ownership, if you check the "false" column frequently, you may want to reconsider whether you would enjoy this line of work.

Traits or Preferences	True	False
I like working with my hands.	❏	❏
I like meeting new people.	❏	❏
I have a tolerance for financial risk.	❏	❏
I enjoy learning about how mechanical things work.	❏	❏
I have a basic knowledge of business and can learn to keep accurate financial records.	❏	❏
I don't mind a fluctuating income from month to month.	❏	❏
Long hours at work don't bother me.	❏	❏
Manual labor isn't a problem for me.	❏	❏
I can work on my own, without a boss to provide direction.	❏	❏
I can deal with the fact that there is great competition in the business.	❏	❏

▲

you need to be someone who stays on top of the industry by reading the trade publications, checking out the car wash-related web sites, and attending seminars, conferences, and trade shows.

The Car Wash That's Right for You

If you haven't done so already, now is the time to think about what type of car wash you want to own. Some of the factors to consider in making your decision include:

- the amount of capital you have at your disposal,
- the amount of time you want to spend running the business, and
- the amount of money you're hoping to make.

In general, the type of car wash that's going to require the biggest investment from you, both in terms of time and money, is a full-service wash. That's also the type that tends to generate the most revenue. But unless you have $1 million or more to invest up front, or can raise that kind of capital from loans and/or investors, it's probably not the best choice. Moving down the line, an exterior-conveyor car wash is the next highest in terms of start-up costs, followed by an in-bay automatic car wash, and finally, a self-service car wash.

Which Car Wash Is Right for You?

Type of Wash	Start-Up Costs	Time Needed	Profit Potential	Required Knowledge
Full-service	High	Intensive	High	Mechanical and general business knowledge a must
Exterior-conveyor	High (somewhat lower labor costs than full-service)	Intensive (slightly lower than full-service)	High	Mechanical and general business knowledge
In-bay automatic	Medium	Medium (significantly less than a full-service or exterior-conveyor car wash)	Medium	Mechanical, some basic knowledge of business practices
Self-service	Low to medium	Low to medium	Low to medium	Mechanical, some basic knowledge of business practices

Each type of car wash has its advantages in terms of time and capital investment vs. profit potential. If your goal is simply to make extra money to supplement another income, consider sticking to a car wash with a few self-service bays—at least initially. If this new business is intended to be your life's pursuit and your primary income, you're probably going to need a full-service or exterior-conveyor car wash to make that happen.

Another factor affecting your decision will be how you plan to start up the business. If you are planning to buy an existing business, you will need capitol, but loans and investors may be easier to find (although it is still difficult) than if you are planning to buy or lease land and build a car wash from the ground up. The chart on the previous page may indicate which car wash is best for you.

How Much Can You Really Make?

You wouldn't be getting into this business if you didn't think there was the opportunity to turn a healthy profit. But how much can you really expect to make? Because we're not discussing a one-size-fits-all business when we talk about a car wash, how much you can make is dependent on a number of factors. Ask yourself the following questions to get a handle on what you can expect:

- *What type of car wash will you operate (exterior-conveyor, full-service, in-bay automatic, or self-service)?* In general, the more services you provide, the more money you're going to make. A full-service car wash, which frequently "upsells" customers, has a higher profit potential than a self-service car wash. Of course, it also requires the biggest investment, costs more to maintain, and is the greatest financial risk.

- *How much business will your location support?* Clearly, a well-traveled, busy area is more likely to do well, while an out-of-the-way location is less likely to draw the same amount of business. Location is important for any business that depends on customers showing up. Of course an out-of-the-way location, may be less expensive to lease or buy and with very good marketing efforts (such as good signage), you can make up the difference.

- *What are the demographics of the area?* Upscale car owners are typically more likely to pay higher prices and even opt for detailing than used car owners or college students.

- *What is the climate like?* In areas that get hit with a lot of snow, car owners may be in more often to clean their cars. In a rainy area, you may have fewer busy days.

Clearly, these are among a variety of factors you will need to consider when deciding where to open a car wash and the kind of car wash to open. Also, the costs of doing

▲

business will vary from region to region based on state and local taxes, utility costs, and other such factors that are out of your control. No matter how you slice it, running a car wash in Manhattan will cost you more than running a car wash in Des Moines.

With all of that being said, here are some general guidelines for the profit potential of the four types of car washes we've mentioned:

1. *Full-service car wash:* $400,000 to $750,000 a year
2. *Exterior-conveyor car wash:* $100,000 to $375,000 a year
3. *In-bay automatic car wash (a "3 and 1 combination" of self-service and in-bay automatic wash bays, discussed in Chapter 4):* $50,000 to $100,000 a year
4. *Self-service car wash (assuming a four-bay, self-service facility):* $40,000 to $80,000 a year

Now that you know the basics of the car wash industry, it's time to move on to the nitty-gritty of running and building your business. In Chapter 2, we'll delve into the foundation of starting your car wash business—carefully researching your market.

Get to Know
Your Market

It's tempting to say that anyone who owns a car, truck, bus, or other motorized vehicle is a potential customer for your car wash. In a sense, that's true. But it's not exactly specific enough to allow you to develop an accurate business plan. Consultants who help car wash entrepreneurs open new businesses ask dozens of questions before passing judgment on the viability of a new site, and they charge a hefty fee for the service. To truly give your-self the best opportunity to succeed, you'll need to ask yourself some of those same questions. Let's start by defining exactly who will make up your customer base.

Who Is the Car Wash Customer?

There are several types of car wash customers. Some you can serve no matter what type of car wash you have, while others will require a car wash with specialized equip-ment if you hope to capture their business. For example, if you want to wash large trucks, you're going to need special equipment designed for this purpose (see the "Oversized Car Washes" section on page 15 for more information).

Here are the various market segments of potential customers and some general information about each:

- *Home washers.* Home washers account for close to 50 percent of the total pub-lic, according to the International Carwash Association (ICA). As you might expect, home washers tend to live in suburban communities and have average incomes. It's also likely that these washers live in single-family homes, where they have space to wash their cars on their own.

  Although the costs associated with hand washing a car at home, both in terms of supplies and time, may make it less economical than getting a bare-bones package at a professional car wash, these "noncustomers" still see doing it themselves as a money-saving proposition.

- *Self-service washers.* The self-service car wash patron is typically a renter. Since they don't own a home and may have little space to wash a car where they live, a professional facility is a necessity. They're also a bit more cost-conscious than those who frequent full-service or exterior-conveyor washes, and tend to have slightly lower incomes. There are also individuals who are concerned about the finish on their cars being scratched or not responding well to the equipment at a full-service wash and prefer the option of using professional equipment, but doing the job themselves.

- *In-bay automatic, exterior-conveyor, and full-service washers.* As you might expect, the typical patron of an auto-matic wash is a bit more affluent than the self-service customer, choosing to pay to have their car washed away from home, even though most are home-owners with space to do it themselves.

Stat Fact
According to a fact sheet from www.carcarecentral.com, 58 percent of home car washers are women.

The ICA goes to great expense to compile statistical data on car wash customers' attitudes and preferences, and these reports are available to ICA members only. The ICA is an organization that you'll probably want to join as soon as possible to gain access to the wealth of information it has accumulated that can help you grow your business.

Finding a Niche

For the most part, you can expect the bulk of your business to come from the traditional source—individual car owners. But there are other market segments that can be profitable as well. Here are a few ideas for how you might be able to serve a special market and fill a niche within the industry.

Fleet Washing

Think about how many types of businesses or government agencies there are that you might be able to target. Police departments, taxi and limousine services, auto rental agencies, and new or used car dealers are just a few of the different organizations that need to wash many cars on a regular basis. If you're creative, you should be able to come up with ways to service these markets, no matter what type of car wash you have.

An agreement to service a fleet of police cruisers, for example, might take one of several forms. You could charge a flat monthly fee and agree to provide a certain number of washes during the month. You could select a certain time of the week that your business is less crowded than normal.

Alternatively, and this is more suited to a self-service or in-bay automatic car wash, you might provide car wash tokens at a discounted price. Another option, for a full-service or exterior-conveyor car wash, is to simply log the number of times a police cruiser uses the wash, and then bill the department each month on a discounted scale. Just about any type of arrangement is possible. The only drawback is that because you're providing discounts, your margins will be smaller. But most car wash owners say the volume more than makes up for it, especially in typically "quiet" hours.

Oversized Car Washes

How many times have you been behind a filthy semi and seen the words "Wash Me" carved out of the dirt and grime. There's a reason for this: Most traditional car washes simply aren't equipped to handle the "big rigs," and you can take advantage of that fact. If you're dead set on opening a car wash but can't find a suitable location, you might want to look into opening a specialty wash that caters to oversized vehicles. Your business model will be somewhat different from the standard car wash that serves the general consumer, but the basics of how you'll succeed are still the same. You'll need to be located where these oversized vehicles travel and preferably stop—perhaps at a rest area along a well-traveled truck route, such as I-95 in the eastern United States.

If you're planning to open this type of car wash, it's very important to make sure any prospective site is able to accommodate the large washing machinery that's required. The easiest and best way to do this is to consult manufacturers of this equipment to find out exactly what you'll need in terms of space.

What Customers Want

No surprise here: a clean car at a fair price in a reasonable amount of time. But what that means might vary depending on the customer. For example, a car owner who has become accustomed to full-service treatment would probably find the process of washing his car at a self-service wash unacceptable. Similarly, a customer used to the relatively quick process involved in an in-bay automatic wash probably won't be happy waiting 15 or 20 minutes for a full-service wash. What this demonstrates is that "a clean car at a fair price in a reasonable amount of time" doesn't necessarily mean the same thing to every customer.

A Clean Car

How you define a clean car and how your customers define a clean car may be different. For some car wash owners, a clean car means whatever the end result is of one trip through the tunnel. For others, especially full-service car wash owners, a clean car means one that is spotless inside and out. Although today's automatic equipment is pretty good, it's probably going to require at least some form of hand washing to get a spotless car. For a self-service washer, a clean car is going to be whatever the owner decides is clean.

You're going to have to decide what degree of clean you'll be aiming for at your car wash. There will be some customers who are never satisfied, while others will be happy as long as your equipment does a decent job. It's how you handle the hard-to-please variety that will define your service.

A Fair Price

In general, the price you charge is going to have to be about the same price others in your area are charging. There's very little you can do to change that. However, you can explore various factors that can make your prices slightly higher or lower than the "going rate" in your area.

Pricing is a matter of putting together various components of your business and punching numbers repeatedly until you have a fair price. You need to factor in the costs

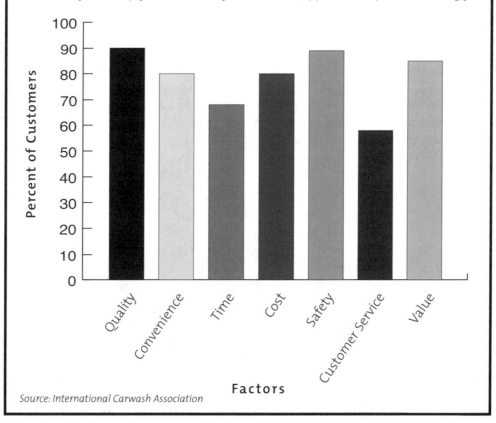

What's Important When Choosing a Wash?

Customers who typically wash their cars at home can be persuaded to let professionals do it instead—but first you'll have to convince them that there's a reason to switch. By knowing the factors that would be most likely to bring a home washer to your shop, you can tailor your services, approach, or price accordingly.

Percent of Customers

Factors

Quality · Convenience · Time · Cost · Safety · Customer Service · Value

Source: International Carwash Association

of doing business, which will vary significantly depending on where you are located and what level of services and amenities you offer. Start with the basics of running the business, including the equipment; soap, detergents, and any other chemicals; labor; and all other essentials. Remember to factor in some marketing/advertising. If you provided no additional services, what could you charge per car and how would that stand up against your competition? Keep in mind that the further away the competition, the less you need to be as closely concerned, since studies show that most drivers go to the nearest car wash, unless there is a specific reason to drive farther to another car wash. Nonetheless, you can't charge $17 if the closest car wash, even a few miles away, is charging $9 for the same level of service.

Stat Fact

According to the International Car-wash Association, for customers who normally visit an exterior-only or stationary-automatic wash, convenience was the most important factor in determining which wash to visit.

Now comes the interesting part, gaining a competitive edge. If pricing is in line with the other car washes in your general region (rural northwest, east coast metropolitan, etc.) and you are looking to gain a following, you can begin adding services that will entice people to your wash. A few small services can bring in more customers at a slightly higher rate. There are simple services that can be added into your tunnel that will not add to your labor cost and will not adversely affect your time of service. According to Sonny's, one of the leading manufacturers of car wash equipment, sealer waxes, tricolor conditioners and protectants, wheel cleaning, and undercarriage wash with rust inhibitor have become proven extras adding from $.12 to $1.00 per service. Promoted on a sign out front and in you advertising, you can easily draw more customers than you will lose by the slightly higher price.

Detailing, and other options, can also add to your price and increase your bottom line. There are also extras that are less car-wash specific, but draw attention. For example, are you located next to a gas station? Perhaps combining services can provide more volume and allow you to charge slightly less for the option of a fill up and a wash. One of the premier ways in which businesses in general are able to charge a little more is by providing quality customer service and attention. This is starting to spill over into the car wash industry. More people will respond to friendly and helpful service than grunts by your car wash attendants. While many people in the industry still suffer from the "what's in it for me" syndrome, attitudes are changing and more car wash owners are becoming aware that their customers are concerned about protecting their own $20,000 to $400,000 investments—their cars. They want their questions answered and their cars treated with care. Therefore, if you care about the customers, they will return, and tell their friends, resulting in more business for the smart car wash owner.

While it's true that for many people a car wash is still just a car wash, you can change that basic attitude by gaining a good or bad reputation. Customers today are no longer just going to show up no matter what—if they are not treated well, they won't return. Remember, 50 percent of car washes are done in driveways. So, there does not need to be a full-service car wash down the road for you to lose business. You are never the only game in town. Therefore, if you drive customers away, you'll need to charge more to stay afloat. Attract more business and you can underprice your competition. That part is simple.

All of this factors into your bottom line and ultimately your pricing.

A Reasonable Amount of Time

Years ago, people thought nothing of waiting 45 minutes or more for a full-service wash to be completed. Today, anything more than 18 minutes and you'll lose business. Saving time is a trend that's continuing just about everywhere. Customers want the same thing they got before, only better and faster.

Estimating how long your customers will view as reasonable depends on what they've come to expect from other washes in your area. If 18 minutes is the average for a full service wash, then you should expect to match that or risk losing customers. If you can beat the average time, it could become one of the major selling points of your business. Of course, it all depends on what service you offer and what customers come to expect from your car wash. The new Express Car washes are getting cars through a shorter tunnel in five minutes or less and provide no detailing or interior services, except perhaps a coin-operated vacuum as an option for the customer. Therefore, the car is getting a fast wash but not the same quality of wash as a full service wash with hands-on detailing. Therefore, time is relative to what you offer your customers.

In addition, the idea of multiprofit centers, which, as discussed earlier, can be anything from actual mini-convenience stores to several vending machines, can be factored into the equation as well. Customers may not find 20 minutes too long to get a quality car wash, while also having the opportunity to pick up a few items that they need. Therefore, the term "reasonable" today means different things to different car wash owners—the bottom line means being competitive in your market and giving people more if they are staying at your facility longer.

For a self-service wash, this concept is turned on its head. People are paying for time in a self-service wash, and they want as much of it as they can get. To compete as a self-service, you're probably going to have to offer at least as much time for each token (dollar, quarter, or whatever) as your competitors. The key to success is making the service as user-friendly as possible, meaning clear instructions, enough room for customers to wash their cars, and a well-kept, clean environment, which will typically mean hiring someone to maintain the premises or doing this job yourself. It also means having all of the self-service equipment in working order at all times.

Value

Here are some things to consider when you ask if you're providing what the typical car wash customer is looking for:

- *How do your prices compare to the competition?* If your competitors are all

Stat Fact

According to the International Carwash Association, customers who typically use a full-service wash say the quality of service is the single most important factor that determines which car wash they use.

offering their services for a substantially cheaper price, you're going to have a hard time satisfying customers, even if you manage to attract them in the first place. In other words, a fair price is relative to what competitors in your area charge for similar services. Remember to compare full service to full service, express to express, and self-serve to self-serve, otherwise you're mixing apples and oranges or perhaps Toyotas to Cadillacs.

Stat Fact
More than 65 percent of conveyor wash owners own only a single location, according to *Professional Carwashing & Detailing* magazine.

- *What is your competitive edge?* If your prices are higher (or even the same as your competition), what are you offering that your competition is not? Speed? Convenience? Amenities? A better wash? Detailing? Are you promoting the selling points of your wash?

Researching Your Market

Market research has become a must for starting a new business. If you don't know who your potential customers are, or don't have an adequate profile of them, then you won't know what to do in order to "win them over."

Here are some of the things you'll want to find out about the market in your area.

- *Your potential customers.* Who are they? What is their average income? Are they homeowners or renters? How many cars does the average family own and are they primarily owned or leased vehicles?

- *Your potential neighborhood.* Is it an area where people routinely come for products and services or is it rundown and off the beaten path? What are the economics of the area? What are the traffic patterns?

- *Your competition.* You'll need to know what kind of competition you'll be up against. What is the closest competition? What is the average cost for a basic exterior wash? What is the most expensive package? What is the average cost of one minute of time (for self-service owners only)? What is the average time for completion of a basic (or full-service) wash cycle? Number of self-service bays or full-service car washes within three miles of your potential business? What additional services do they offer (i.e. waxing, vacuuming, etc.)? What extra amenities do they offer (i.e. greeters, vending machines, convenience products, etc.)?

We've provided a Market Research Checklist for you to use while gathering information on the market in your area. You will also want to refer to this checklist as you read through the next chapter, which deals with researching and choosing a location for your business.

Compiling Such Data

Sure, it's easy to say that you should compile all sorts of data about your potential customers and the area in which you hope to open business, but how do you go about this?

You may start by using some primary research, which is research you gather yourself. Questionnaires, telephone surveys, and even informal marketing groups, whereby you invite two dozen local citizens to a free breakfast or lunch in exchange for an hour of talk about the need for a new car wash—or not—are potentially very valuable. You can also interview other business owners (not competitors) who can give you a very

Market Research Checklist

Here is some of the information you'll need to know about your market.

Information to Gather	Check When Done
Population within two miles of car wash site?	
Population within three miles of car wash site?	
Population within five miles of car wash site?	
Traffic flow: How many cars pass by your proposed site on an average day?	
Traffic patterns: What is the speed limit on the adjacent road?	
Housing: Comprised mainly of single-family homes or apartment buildings?	
Street location: Corner or midblock?	
Competition: Number of car washes within three miles of your site?	
Amenities: Number of convenience stores or other businesses in the immediate area?	
Labor pool: Is there an adequate source of labor in your neighborhood?	
Average household income within three miles of your site?	

▲

good feel for the neighborhood. Ask if you can sit in at a meeting of local business owners or at a chamber of commerce meeting and introduce yourself. These are people with which you will want to build alliances.

The other means of finding out more about your potential area of business is by doing secondary research, which means using the library, the internet, and existing sources to gather data.

Great sources of secondary data include:

- www.epodunk.com: Neighborhood profiles and data

- http://stats.bls.gov: The Bureau of Labor Statistics

- www.busreslab.com: Business Research Lab

- www.fedstats.gov: Federal statistics

- www.census.gov: The United States Census Bureau

- You might also look for *Gale's Business Directory* in your local library.

In addition, you should look at local area web sites for local statistical information and trends.

Of course, all the data isn't worth the paper this page is printed on if you do not sit down and evaluate it carefully. Neither this book nor any car wash consultant can determine whether or not you could, or should, open a car wash. Only you can use your market research data (particularly the local data) to determine the best route to take based on your findings. Don't be scared to sit down with your accountant to punch up the numbers based on your data. Also remember to consider what your goals are for entering the business. Is this a full-time business or a part-time endeavor to add additional income? Factor your goals in with the research you have done.

Location, Location, Location

Whether you're talking about office space, a hotel, a supermarket, or a car wash, location is typically one of the most important factors (if not the most important) in creating a successful business. "I've known a lot of bad car washes in good locations that have done very well," says one car

▲

wash consultant we interviewed. "And I've known a lot of great car washes that have been in poor locations that didn't do well."

In the car wash business, a good location can mean many different things. First of all, the location has to be a good match for the type of car wash you're operating. For example, a full-service car wash will generally be a better fit for a more upscale community, where there are lots of owners of expensive cars who are willing to spend a little more money to keep them clean. A self-service wash might be a better fit for a community where car owners are more cost-conscious.

There are a number of factors that you will need to explore when seeking a location to build a car wash. If you are looking to buy one, the location has already been chosen for the purpose of such a business. However, you may need to determine if the location is still as promising for business as it was when the seller first set up shop. Therefore, you will also have to evaluate the location because neighborhoods change, along with zoning laws, traffic patterns, and various other factors. What was a marvelous place to open a car wash 20 years ago may not be the ideal place to run one today.

Here are some of the factors you will need to consider when evaluating a prospective site.

Local Government

The local zoning laws of the community and the support you can expect to receive from the local government and residents are crucial factors in your site-selection process. In fact, this is listed first because it is the first thing you need to consider before even starting your location search.

Typically, car washes are zoned into business areas, but not always.

In many cases, car washes still suffer from the public perception that they are somehow "seedy" businesses that employ drifters and bring an unwanted element into a community. Although this isn't really the case, old attitudes and prejudices die hard.

Nonetheless, for whatever reason, if the area is not zoned for a car wash, you can either fight city hall (which can be a long running battle) or move on to another location. If it is zoned for a car wash, you will have other variables to consider that we will discuss below. However, you will at least have a place to consider.

Another, very common possibility is that you will need a variance or special permit to open a car wash in a specific area. This can be tricky, and you will need an attorney to determine exactly what is and is not permitted and who (if anyone) can come in and change the rules on you in a month, a year, or a few years. Many owners have had to put up with years of haggling and legal battles just to win the right to open a new car wash. Often times they simply give up, figuring that the fight isn't worth whatever they might potentially gain from owning the business. This may be what some local government officials are banking on—if they make it hard enough, word will get out that it's more trouble than it's worth to open a car wash in their area. Of course, if you jump all of the hurdles and have a long range plan (and can afford to wait awhile), you may be in good shape. Because if you do get approval, it is highly unlikely that you will have any competition.

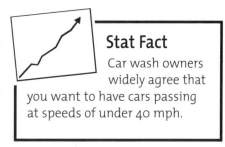

Stat Fact
Car wash owners widely agree that you want to have cars passing at speeds of under 40 mph.

You will need to investigate the zoning regulations carefully. To do so, you should consult the local planning board and even get an area zoning map. Of course, even if the area is zoned for a car wash, there may still be other zoning regulations that can impact upon your decision. For example, let's say that you have found a prime location just off a busy roadway. Local zoning regulations may require that you have an inordinate amount of space to account for waiting lines, which could scuttle your initial plans for the size of your site and how much of it can be used for actual wash bays. Another potential problem involves roadway expansion. It has happened that potential owners have seen their lot size effectively and dramatically decreased because the local government wanted to keep the option of widening the road at some unspecified date in the future. The lesson? Before you invest your time and money in a new site, make sure the powers that be won't throw you a curve ball.

There's yet another way the government can scuttle your car wash plans before they get started, and this involves impact fees. The way they see it, your car wash is going to affect the surrounding environment. And by environment, we don't mean the air and water, although water runoff is a concern. However, in this case, what they're most likely going to be talking about is the roadway. Depending on where you choose to set up shop, you could be hit with a penalty of sorts because of the number of cars the local government expects to come to you for a wash. The theory is that were your wash not there, those cars wouldn't travel the roadway and wouldn't contribute to the wear and tear on the asphalt. In essence, because of you, the road is going to deteriorate just a bit faster than it would have if people stayed home to wash their cars. Whether or not this is true really doesn't matter. If they say it's so, then it's so, and you'd better plan on getting out your checkbook.

The Land Itself or the Building

A great parcel of land on the perfect corner is not going to support a car wash if it's on the side of a hill, is too small, or has serious drainage problems. If you're building a full-service car wash, you'll need land (preferably rectangular) that can accommodate the structure, the cars waiting, and the cars being dried, plus perhaps a storage area and parking for your employees. If you are buying an existing car wash, you will need to evaluate not only the location but also the condition of the

building. The best location may not be so wonderful if the existing car wash is ready to fall down. More on buying a car wash vs. building one later on.

Traffic Flow

There's an old saying about a successful salesman that says, "He could sell ice to an Eskimo." You may be that type of person. You may be the greatest salesman in the world, but if you're trying to sell car wash services in an area where there are no cars, you're going to have a problem. Generally, the most successful washes are located on busy (but not incredibly fast-moving) thoroughfares.

Before you even think about designing your car wash, you'll want to scout several possible locations and measure the traffic flow. How many cars pass by each hour? When is the traffic heaviest? If you're doing the study yourself, you may want to actually stand on the site and watch the cars drive by to see what types of cars the people are driving. Do this a few times and you'll begin to get an idea of which type of wash the area might support. If you're buying an existing wash, this data will probably be available from the previous owner. Don't just take his word for it, look for statistics on a long-term basis. If you're planning to build one, you'll have to come up with this information on your own.

Local government agencies may also be another source for information on traffic flow. For example, you might try contacting your city's or state's planning commission to see if it has traffic-flow data. The department should be able to provide you with information that will give you a good idea of how many cars generally pass by your site on any given day. Do whatever you have to get an accurate estimate of this—it's one of the most important factors regarding the viability of a car wash business.

Along with the traffic flow, you also have to consider the possibility of cars making a turn into your car wash. Can cars from the opposite side of the road make the turn without causing potential accidents? Is there a turning lane? Is there a median preventing them from even getting to your car wash? Along with the flow of traffic, you need to consider the traffic laws and accessibility.

Traffic Speed

Perhaps just as important as the number of cars that pass by your location is how fast the cars are going. Drivers moving along at 25 to 35 mph are more likely to see your sign and either decide to pull in and have their car washed or make a mental note to return later than those whizzing by at 55. A road with traffic lights or stop signs can be beneficial because drivers are forced to slow down more frequently, thus enabling them to see your business more easily. Keep in mind that many people pull into a car wash on an impulse, simply determining that they have some spare time and a relatively dirty car.

Street Location and Visibility

Ideally, you'd like to be located on a busy corner with a stoplight on a heavily traveled road. The traffic light forces cars to stop and gives drivers ample opportunity to pull into your wash. You also want to have easy access to your car wash, preferably with a driveway right off the road. This should be something you're able to determine simply by driving the road yourself. If you can answer "yes" to the question, "Is this location easy and convenient for cars on this road to see and get to?" then it's probably a good location. Before buying a lot or an existing car wash,

Capture Caper

Your capture rate—the percentage of cars that drive by your wash and actually stop to patronize your business—is one of the most important statistics for any car wash owner. There are many factors that will affect your capture rate, including the speed limit, the presence of traffic lights or stop signs, your visibility from the road, the ease of entrance and exit from your lot, and the presence of other businesses that help to keep drivers alert to what's available along the side of the road.

Once you know the average traffic flow each day you can expect, then you need to turn your attention to determining the capture rate you can expect. This information will help you get a solid idea of just how many customers you can expect every day. If you're buying an existing car wash, the current owner should be able to provide this information. A recent survey by *Professional Carwashing & Detailing* magazine found that capture rates ranged from 0.45 percent for exterior-only conveyor washes to 0.52 percent for full-service washes. That was significantly lower than numbers reported the previous year (0.76 percent for exterior-only and 0.56 percent for full-service).

To use your capture rate to compute an average number of customers a day, multiply the traffic count by your anticipated capture rate. For example:

20,000 cars a day x .0045 *(representing a 0.45 percent capture rate)* =
90 customers a day

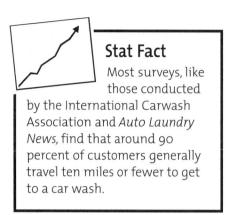

Stat Fact

Most surveys, like those conducted by the International Carwash Association and *Auto Laundry News,* find that around 90 percent of customers generally travel ten miles or fewer to get to a car wash.

determine the visibility of the car wash from the road. As you drive up to it, is it blocked from your view by other businesses? Other buildings? Anything obscuring a driver's view of your business will limit your capture rate. You will also want to check in with local government agencies and find out if anything is about to be constructed alongside of the car wash or the lot on which you intend to build.

Signage

You should first check with the local government to determine what you will legally be allowed to construct. There may be restrictions on sign height or type of sign (neon lights, sign with a menu of services, etc.). Large signs that dominate the landscape might not be permitted in some areas. In other areas, this may not be a problem as long as you meet certain requirements. The only way to find out is to check the regulations beforehand.

Assuming that the laws aren't too restrictive, the next step is to determine what kind of signage the site can support and where it will be visible to drivers on the road. You'll want to have enough space to construct your sign in an area that maximizes its visibility to drivers. Preferably, the sign should be visible from 250 to 300 feet away. If you're behind a building, around a sharp bend in the road, or some other less-than-ideal situation, you might find that no matter what kind of sign you construct, it's going to be nearly impossible for your potential customers to spot. Try walking along the road, rather than driving it, so you can see in more detail exactly where the blind spots might be. All other things being equal, the better site is the one that gives your car wash maximum exposure. Some car washes have fared very well in locations where the actual wash was blocked by other buildings, but the large sign was not. In fact, rent may be cheaper if you take a spot that is behind a retail outlet, but has excellent signage and ample space.

The Competition

Is there another car wash right across the street from the site you're considering? Is there one down the road? Is there one at the corner a short distance away, while your site is in the middle of a block? These are obvious factors you'll want to consider when evaluating a site. But there are other, more subtle ones as well.

For example, is there a gas station nearby? Even if they do not offer car washes yet, they certainly may in the future. Is there a lube shop or car repair center? Again, more potential competitors. We're not saying that the mere presence of competition will kill your car wash. Maybe, with a combination of better service and better prices, you could win the battle for customers. But if it's a choice between two otherwise promising sites—one with no competition and one with plenty of competition—it should be an easy choice. Of course, a good entrepreneur might also see an opportunity and cross-promote with the gas station or the repair business. You send them customers and they send customers to you.

Stat Fact
According to a recent survey from *Auto Laundry News,* more than 50 percent of car wash owners reported having more than two competitors in their area.

Neighborhood Demographics

Different types of washes can, and do, succeed in different types of communities. Whether or not the community you're considering is right for the type of car wash you want to open is a matter of some background research. Start by determining what type of wash you'll be able to operate given the space you have available. It may be that you simply don't have enough room for the kind of car wash that fits the community.

You'll also want to look at the type of housing that exists in the area surrounding your prospective site. Generally, apartment complexes are better than single-family housing. This is true for a couple of reasons. First, lots of apartment buildings mean you have a higher population density in the area. Second, apartment-dwellers generally don't have a driveway or access to an outside water source to wash their cars. This segment of the market is usually obligated to visit a professional car wash—or else let their cars stay dirty.

Weather

This variable will have more to do with the area of the country in which you locate your car wash rather than the area of town where you put down stakes. People don't wash their cars when it's raining—that much is clear. So if you plan on opening your wash in a rainy climate, you may have more days of slow business than if you settled in a drier climate.

This doesn't mean car washes can't be successful all over the country. There are plenty of successful car wash businesses in Seattle, just as there are plenty of successful car wash businesses in Los Angeles, but it is a factor to keep in mind.

Not surprisingly, surveys show that the best time of year for most car washes is in the winter. Road salt, snow, slush, and the other side effects of inclement weather that occur in the northern half of the country make this a boom time for many businesses. In warmer, sunnier climates, you may benefit from the fact that there are fewer rainy days to cut into your business. In the end, it might be a trade-off, but the weather is a factor to consider when you develop your business plan.

Smart Tip

Don't give up on a location just because it's in a low-income area. For just about any community, there's a type of wash that's right, which in this case may mean self-serve as opposed to full-service.

Proximity to Other Amenities

The majority of today's car wash customers want to combine a trip to the car wash with an opportunity to run other errands. In surveys, more customers say they would rather combine the act of getting a car wash with getting a tank of gas than any other errand. If you happen to be located near or even right next to a busy gas station, you may have a partner working for you to pull customers in to your location. Some car wash owners have worked out arrangements with gas stations to give reduced-price washes with any fill-up or when a certain amount of gas is purchased. Convenience stores are also helpful at drawing business. You may be are able to work out an arrangement in which the store gives discount coupons for washes to its customers. Even if you wind up paying for the entire discount, it can keep a steady flow of cars coming through your wash.

Labor Pool

Unless you're operating only the smallest of self-service washes, you're probably going to need to hire employees. This means you're going to need an available pool of qualified job candidates. We'll get into more detail about what to look for in employees in Chapter 8, but for now it's important to think about what kind of workers you'll have available in your particular area. If you suspect there will be a shortage of people willing to work at a car wash in your area, recognize that you're probably going to have to pay more for labor and that you may have a harder time finding workers no matter how much you're willing to pay.

It's a plus if you're located in an area where the traditional sources of car wash labor are also located—for example, if there's a college or high school nearby. If you see many fast-food restaurants or convenience stores in your area, two other businesses that typically employ unskilled workers, that's a pretty good indication that potential employees are around. Though it can also mean you'll have to compete with these other businesses for good workers.

Power and Utilities

Electricity, water, and gas are a few things you will need to operate a business, particularly a car wash. Who services the area? What are the costs? These are important factors, because the high cost of utilities can knock out any possible profit. Steve Gaudreau, car wash consultant and president of the Car Wash College™, (see

Appendix) recommends getting a good reclaim system installed to help you save on water costs. More about how a reclaim system works is found later in the discussion of car washes and the environment.

Now that we've discussed what to look for when you're scouting potential locations, let's turn to how you'll run the business you're going to build. In Chapter 4, you'll learn about the general tasks involved in running a car wash business.

4

Running
Your Business

Most car wash owners say there really
isn't a typical day that can be applied across the board. How you
run your business day to day will depend on some of the key decisions you make when you're starting out. For example, will this
business be your sole source of income? Will you be operating a
full-service car wash or a self-service car wash?

If you decide on a self-service car wash, how many bays will you have? Will they all be in one location, or will they be spread around town? These are all factors that will eventually determine what your day will be like as a car wash owner.

A Day in the Life

Up to this point, we've been discussing the four distinct types of car washes. In this chapter, we'll combine them into just two categories—conveyor (which includes exterior-only and full-service washes) and self-serve (which includes true self-service wand bays and in-bay automatic roll-over units)—because many of the responsibilities overlap. For example, the owner of a conveyor wash that provides exterior cleaning only is going to have a similar typical day to the owner of a conveyor wash that includes interior cleaning services, too.

The Conveyor Car Wash Owner

Assuming that you're running the business yourself, as the owner of a full-service wash or an exterior-conveyor wash you'll first go into the "office" (most likely a small room at your wash) to coordinate the day's events. Based on a number of factors, including the weather, the season, and the day of the week, you'll have to make some decisions about the number of employees you'll need that day and when you'll need them. If you had planned on having only half a dozen employees in that day because the weatherman predicted rain, you'll have to round up some extra workers if it turns out to be bright and sunny. If the opposite happens—unexpected bad weather—you're going to have to reschedule some employees or find something else for them to do (if you're lucky, something that contributes to your sales).

The next task is to make sure that your equipment is operating as it should be. Is the machinery functioning properly? Are there any manual changes or decisions that you might want to make that day? For example, depending on the anticipated flow of traffic, based on the weather, the day of the week (weekends are obviously busier) and other factors, you might want to speed up or slow down the conveyor speed slightly. If it looks like a slow day, you can slow down the conveyor—the result being a better wash, since cars will receive that much more detergent and will come out sparkling. Therefore, you may earn less money on such a day, but those customers that you do get will be impressed and be back again. Of course on a very busy day, rather that having people waiting in long lines, you may speed up the conveyor, getting more cars through and increasing sales, at the expense of as clean a wash. There are a number of these types of decisions that you will find yourself making as you familiarize yourself with the equipment. The FlexServe system for running a wash promotes the idea of flexibility and leaving yourself some options in how you determine which aspects of full-service you do and do not want to include.

Do you have all of the necessary supplies? You may need to call your suppliers or send an employee that is not busy over to pick up something that you need. Additionally, you may encounter a mechanical problem that you can't fix on your own. You'll have to contact your repair person—and fast—or risk losing significant business.

Once open, your day will probably be spent monitoring the wash. Some owners like to be very accessible to their customers, chatting up regulars because most businesses—car washes included—operate on an 80-20 principal, meaning that 80 percent of your business comes from regular customers and 20 percent from new customers. Of course, you'll also want to introduce yourself to new customers, if possible, and build a bond so that they'll choose your wash over a competitor's.

There's a very good chance that you'll have to do some troubleshooting as well. No matter how good your equipment and employees are, there are going to be problems during a typical day. There are some cars that a fully automated, exterior-conveyor wash just cannot clean to the owner's satisfaction. There are stories of owners with off-road vehicles, caked with mud and grime, visiting a car wash after a session of "four wheeling" and complaining that one run through the tunnel failed to clean the car. You, as the owner, are going to hear about it when something like that happens. Is there a scratch on the car that was clearly there before it ran through your wash, which the owner of the car blames you for anyway? These are all situations you'll encounter if not every day, at least on a regular basis. What you decide your customer service policy is going to be will in large part dictate how you interact with customers on a daily basis. Will it be "We're not satisfied until you're satisfied," or "We cannot be held responsible for damage to your car"?

Depending on how many employees you have, at the end of the day you may spend some time counting and distributing tips to your "send-off" employees (the people who dry off the car at the end of the cycle) or computing commissions for your service writers.

After everyone else has gone home, there's still some work left for you to do. (Hey, it's lonely at the top.) You're probably going to want to do a rundown of the day's business. How many cars passed through? Was it significantly more or less than you had expected? If it was significantly busier, you'll want to try to figure out why. Was it something you did, or was it luck? Was it some brilliant stroke of marketing genius? And speaking of marketing, how did your efforts pay off? How many coupons did you redeem today? Where did they come from? By evaluating your marketing efforts, you can determine if they are paying off and in what part of town.

If business was a bit slower than you expected, what can you do to improve? Assuming the weather was good and there weren't any other extenuating circumstances, there must have been some other problem, right? Maybe, maybe not. But it's almost a guarantee that you'll think about it long after everyone else is at home with their families.

After you're done analyzing the day's events, it's time to check the equipment and supplies again, and get ready for tomorrow. You'll want to know what supplies you are running low on and what you need to order for tomorrow.

You may listen to the weather report to see if you're going to have to adjust your staffing to compensate for better- or worse-than-expected weather.

You may likely stop and make a deposit at the bank, and when all that is done, you're done. And you get to look forward to coming in bright and early the next day and doing it all over again.

The Self-Serve Car Wash Owner

As the owner of a self-service or an in-bay-automatic car wash, you'll face some of the same challenges of a conveyor wash owner, but on a somewhat smaller scale. And some of the issues conveyor owners deal with, you won't have to worry about at all.

The typical day in the life of a self-serve owner is going to vary greatly depending on the size of your operation. We'll start by following the hypothetical owner of a mid-sized self-serve—a "3 and 1 combination," or a wash with three self-service bays and one in-bay automatic. Once you see what that's like, then we'll discuss what life is like for the car wash mogul—the owner with a large self-serve facility or one who has several washes dotted around town.

If you have a small operation, you may not have any employees. So that's one headache gone. But guess what, there's another one right there to take its place. If you

---

Doing Away with Graffiti

From time to time, you're probably going to walk into your wash and be greeted by graffiti. Even if your car wash is located in a peaceful, low-crime area, your bay walls are sometimes going to be defaced. Cleaning this stuff up is a hassle. Most hardware stores sell spray-on graffiti removers that you can buy. You can also try some other products, such as Klenztone, made by K&E Chemical Co. Inc. in Cleveland, which is supposed to work on brick.

One car wash owner in Southern California uses chlorine on his concrete walls to clean the grime and bacteria that tends to accumulate in most places that are wet all the time. For graffiti, this same owner has had some success using carburetor cleaner—available for probably less than two bucks at most hardware and auto supply stores. Other products that some owners have recommended are NU-Wall, made by Arcadian, and Clean-Up, made by Blue Coral. Keep trying various products until you find one that works best on your type and color of walls.

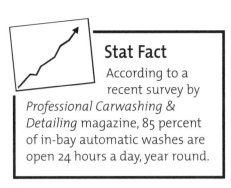

Stat Fact
According to a recent survey by *Professional Carwashing & Detailing* magazine, 85 percent of in-bay automatic washes are open 24 hours a day, year round.

have no employees, it's certainly true that just about everything involved in running a business is easier. Payroll's a snap (since it's nonexistent). Record keeping is much simpler, and there are a whole host of rules and regulations surrounding the hiring and firing of employees that you simply don't have to concern yourself with. But remember, all those things that employees would do if you had them now have to be done by you. Additionally, you will have fewer concerns about equipment since you are not depending on $400,000 worth of full-service conveyor equipment to work efficiently. Of course, you will still need to have the self-serve and in-bay equipment working properly.

So how do you start your day? Here's a hint: You're probably not going to want to wear your nice shoes, because you're probably going to start your day cleaning up. Self-serve car washes, especially if they're open 24/7, get dirty. And people don't want to wash their cars at a dirty car wash.

There are lots of things that need to be cleaned at a self-serve wash. First and foremost are the bays themselves. Not surprisingly, when dirty cars get washed, they leave some dirt behind. You don't want your customers to take one look inside your bays and decide to go to the other car wash a mile away. One of your first duties of the day will be to wash down your bays. You may not have to clean your bays every day, but you should certainly expect to clean them once a week. You'll also probably have to deal with mold or mildew that will accumulate on your walls periodically.

After the bays are cleaned, you're going to have walk around your facility and pick up any miscellaneous garbage that might be lying around. One thing to keep in mind here is that the amount of garbage that's going to accumulate is going to vary depending on the number of vending machines you choose to install. (If you elect to supplement your sales in this way, see Chapter 9 for more information.) Empty soda cans or candy wrappers may be a nuisance, but considering the money you're going to be making from your vending machines, it's probably worth it.

Weather may not play as big a role in your day-to-day operations because, no matter if it's a sunny day or torrential rain, your operation can essentially remain open without incurring the added costs of employees standing around doing nothing. This assumes, of course, that you're managing the operation on your own. If, however, you have an employee whose job it is to remain at the wash, help customers with questions, or deal with complaints, then you will have to make some decisions about how much help you'll need on any given day.

The next thing you're going to have to do is collect your money. Theft is always a concern, and money left in the machines at your wash is bait for thieves. When you actually make the rounds to collect money, keep this guideline in mind: Most owners

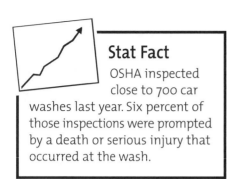

of self-serves advise against developing a routine or pattern that potential criminals can pick up on. For example, if you always show up at 8 A.M. to collect the money, someday you may find a thief waiting right behind you when you're finished.

Then, just like a conveyor owner would, you have to check your equipment and supplies. Because you probably aren't going to be on-site the entire time your wash is operational, you're going to have check for little things that may have gone wrong during the time you were away. Are all of the lights functional? Has a careless customer broken some minor piece of equipment? Are any cash machines or dispensers not working properly? These are the kinds of things you'll be looking for.

Although it may sound like this is easier work than managing a full-service or exterior-conveyor wash, that's not always true. Some self-serve owners with lots of bays to take care of can wind up working harder and longer than their conveyor owner counterparts. But as a general rule, you can probably expect to spend a bit less time running a self-serve car wash business.

What Are Your Goals?

Which path you choose—the more relaxed structure of a self-serve wash or the more intense management of a conveyor wash—is entirely up to you. You may be constrained by start-up capital, which can be close to $2 million for a full-service car wash. As an alternative, you may be forced into the more modest expense of opening a few self-service bays. Bear in mind, however, that your goals should play just as important a role in your decision as your financial ability to invest the capital.

We've mentioned before that you probably can't make a very comfortable living operating a few self-service bays and nothing else. This isn't the case with a full-service wash that offers detailing, lube jobs, oil changes, gasoline, a gift shop, and any number of services or products that help boost the bottom line. Keep that in mind if you plan to start small because it may be some time before you're able to truly quit your day job.

Safety

Along with cleanliness, safety always has to be paramount in your mind. With all that water around, it's important that you take steps to guard against ice and slippery conditions, especially in colder climates. You and your employees will also be working with chemicals—some of which can be harmful. We're not talking so much about the materials used to clean cars, but some of the cleaning solutions you'll be forced to use on your bays to remove graffiti or mold and mildew. Make sure that you and your employees use these chemicals properly, and that you take the appropriate precautions to prevent any safety mishaps. Also make sure you are insured at all times. Do not let your coverage lapse.

One of the consequences of not paying attention to safety and cleanliness can be a lawsuit. Here's an example of what can happen: A woman slipped and fell on some standing water at a car wash and claimed she injured her back. Of course, she decided to sue the owner. While that case was pending, another lawsuit was filed, this time by the woman's husband. It seems that the woman's back was hurt so badly, that the loving couple could no longer . . . well, you know. The husband sued the car wash owner for "loss of affection" because of his wife's injury.

It sounds outrageous. It sounds silly. It sounds like it could never happen to you. But believe it or not, people like to sue. In this day of litigation fever, there are more than $88 billion paid out every year by small business owners to settle cases in or out of court and pay for attorney fees. Think about that the next time you take chances about cleaning up water or other potential hazards. It's worth saying one more time— be insured and stay insured.

Beware!
Everything your customers touch needs to be inspected at least once a day. For example, if a careless customer smears grease on the nozzle of a vacuum, your next customer is going to get that grease all over her car's upholstery, and won't be very happy about it.

Setting Up
Shop

Now that you have a good handle on just

what to expect when running your business, you can start to

make some educated decisions about how to set up your busi-

ness. There are lots of things to consider such as:

- What form your business will take (i.e., corporation,

   sole proprietor, partnership).

- Which experts you will establish relationships with.
- Whether to buy, lease, or build your car wash.
- What type of insurance you will need.
- Whether you will buy or build a car wash.
- What regulatory issues you will have to address.
- The environmental concerns.
- What you will name your business.
- Writing your business plan.

What Form Should Your Business Take?

Very early on in the process of starting your new car wash, you're going to have to make a decision about what form your business should take. Will it be a sole proprietorship? A corporation? Limited liability company? Partnership? For this decision, you should definitely consult with your accountant and a lawyer who is familiar with business law. You will need to sit with your attorney and discuss the implications of each type of business structure and determine which is best for your personal needs.

If you incorporate, you can shield your personal assets from the risk of lawsuits. While this is not always 100 percent the case, it does take the onus off of your personal assets should someone get injured on your property and decide to sue. By incorporating, the business becomes a separate entity and the individual can sue the business as opposed to suing you as an individual, thus allowing you to better protect your personal assets.

Along with the advantages to incorporating comes more paperwork, more record-keeping, and many more technical details to take care of—that's one reason you can't make this decision without some expert advice. There are a number of requirements that must be made within your state to maintain a corporation.

Many entrepreneurs start their businesses as a sole proprietorship or as a partnership. Let's talk a little about these two business structures. One of the biggest advantages to forming a business as a sole proprietorship is that it's easy to do. Basically, the only work you're going to have to do is to obtain whatever general business licenses are required by your city or state to allow you to start doing business. This form of business structure is probably going to be the easiest for you to deal with when it comes time to pay your taxes. Generally, the income from the business is considered personal income, and you simply attach a Schedule C Form as part of a standard 1040 form. You will be able to write off much of your income as business expenses and very likely be able to take many legitimate deductions. While there is less hassle involved in terms of formalities and paperwork, there is also a downside. With a sole proprietorship, you are the business. This means if someone slips and falls on a patch of ice in one of your wash bays, you're the one who's going to pay for it, not a separate corporate entity. This could potentially raise your insurance costs and wreak havoc on your personal assets.

If you're going into the business with a partner, you're probably going to need a partnership agreement. This is a little more complicated than a sole proprietorship, but is still easier to set up than a corporation. You get some of the same advantages with a partnership that you do with a sole proprietorship—ease of setup, no bureaucratic decision-making process, and a direct income from your business. However, there is a downside. At least one of you is still going to be completely personally liable for all the risks associated with a business. Another problem occurs when one partner decides he or she wants out of your partnership. You would then have to restructure the business as a sole proprietorship or find another partner. But perhaps the biggest disadvantage is that you generally have to stand by any agreements your partner makes. That can be dangerous if your partner isn't someone you completely trust.

Limited liability corporations, or LLC's, sometimes provide the best of both worlds as somewhat of a "hybrid" solution. The owners of a LLC have the liability protection of a corporation. Just like a corporation, the LLC exists as a separate entity. Unlike corporations, however, which typically need to file minutes of board meetings and do a lot of paperwork, there are fewer requirements with an LLC. A couple of the drawbacks are that an LLC dissolves when one partner dies or goes bankrupt, where a corporation can go on forever. Also, they are more complex to set up than a sole proprietorship or a partnership, but less complicated than starting a corporation. Additionally, they are not possible in all states, so you will have to find out about an LLC in your state of business.

As we said above, this really isn't a decision you should make without consulting an attorney who can take into account your particular circumstances and recommend the structure that's right for you.

Smart Tip

Tip...

If you want your neighbors to see you as an upstanding member of the community, be sure to give something back. Consider donating money to the local Boy or Girl Scouts, or other community organizations. Perhaps you will consider buying ads in local school newspapers or yearbooks. Not only will it help people remember your name, but it can also give you an edge in the community should you need to change, modify, or oppose local regulations with the potential to hurt your business. Basically, it's easier to fight city hall if you have some friends there.

The Experts

No man is an island. To give yourself the best chance of succeeding in your new business, you're going to need to establish relationships with a stable of experts—people you can call on to deal with situations that will inevitably arise in the course of doing business. Here are some of the professionals you'll need to consult at start-up, and potentially from time to time after that.

Legal Eagles

It should go without saying that you will need someone to handle your legal affairs. You should be able to perform more mundane tasks, such as getting a business license, but while setting up a business, reading through a lease or purchase agreement, or should you ever be sued, you certainly will want to have a lawyer at your side. Your lawyer can also offer advice on how to set up your car wash to avoid potential legal conflicts and can advise you on the form of business (sole proprietorship, corporation, etc.) that would be best for you. To find a qualified attorney, start with the American Bar Association (www.aba.org) or your local city or state's bar association. Look for someone who is familiar with car wash ownership. You might also consult the local car wash association in your state and see if anyone can recommend the name of a good business attorney. Keep in mind that you need an attorney with a business background—meaning that if your brother-in-law, the divorce attorney, wants to do you a favor and "help you out," he may not be the best person for the job—*thanks, but no thanks.*

Number-Crunchers

You don't necessarily need an accountant, but it certainly wouldn't be a bad idea. When you become a business owner, your taxes are going to become more complicated really fast. A reliable accountant handling these things frees you up to focus on growing your business. An accountant can also help you find ways to reduce those taxes and help you keep on track with your business budget. There are several places you can check to find an accountant you're comfortable with. Try the National Association of Small Business Accountants (www.smallbiz accounts.com), the American Institute of Certified Public Accountants (www.aicpa.org), and the National Association of Insurance and Financial Advisors (www.naifa.org). See the Appendix for additional contact information.

> ### Fun Fact
> Did you know that when you buy your car wash you'll be a colleague of Lenny Dykstra, the former Philadelphia Phillies' and New York Mets' great? Dykstra owns a car wash chain.

Insurance Agents

Having an insurance expert who takes the time to understand your particular situation and develops a plan that gives you the right coverage without selling you policies you don't need is vital. Don't even think about opening without first consulting an insurance professional. You can start your search at the Independent Insurance Agents of America (www.iiaa.org) or the National Association of Professional Insurance Agents (www.pianet.com).

Repairpersons

Because so much of your business relies on keeping all that machinery up and running, you're going to need a capable repairperson to handle problems if you can't handle them yourself. The distributor who sold you your equipment might be a good place to start looking for one, as that company will often service the equipment it sells you. In other cases the manufacturer of the equipment may send a rep to repair its equipment. If you're buying an existing car wash, you might want to stick with the same person the previous owner used, since he or she will probably know the equipment inside and out and you may be able to pick up on an existing service agreement.

Architects

You're only going to need an architect if you're building a brand-new wash or are planning extensive renovations to an existing structure. Obviously, not every architect is going to be the right person to design a car wash, so you may have to do some searching. Ask fellow owners if they can recommend someone or check with an organization such as The National Council of Architectural Registration Boards (www. ncarb.org) to find information on licensed architects in your state. Your distributor, supplier, and equipment manufacturer can also probably recommend a qualified professional with car wash experience.

Consultants

No, you do not necessarily need a car wash consultant, but since there are so many details to running such a business and many people who have done this prior to you, it's often a very good idea to tap into their years of experience. A car wash consultant can help you with the nuances that you won't find unless you are in the trenches, so to speak, running an actual car wash. There are some consultants listed in the resource section of the book. Any consultant you find should pay for himself in additional business down the road.

Should You Lease or Buy Your Land?

One of the questions you're probably going to face if you decide to open a new car wash is whether to lease or buy your land. There are many factors that will come into play as you make this decision. Most owners you talk to will say that it's better to own the land your car wash is on rather than lease it. But in some cases, it may be impossible to buy the land. Perhaps the parcel you've targeted for your business isn't for sale. Perhaps you're not a good candidate to buy the land, either because you lack the required capital to purchase it outright or lending companies aren't willing to lend you enough money to make the purchase and build your wash. In short, there might be any number of reasons why leasing makes a lot of sense. First, let's talk a little about how much land you're going to need.

The Size of Your Lot

Before you decide what land to buy, you need to know how much land is required for the type of car wash you want to open. Car wash consultant Steve Gaudreau says that you will need at least three-quarter acre of land that meets the setback and green space requirements of the area in which you are planning to start the business. "Most conveyor car washes are built on an acre or more, but you can get by with slightly less," says Gaudreau, who along with owning his Massachusetts-based consulting business, is also president of the Car Wash College (see Appendix). In-bay and self-serve car washes will require less space.

Stat Fact
According to a recent report from the International Carwash Association, 76 percent of full-service car wash owners have a gift shop as an added profit center.

For a conveyor system, along with the actual tunnel you're generally going to need a lot that provides sufficient area for cars to wait and for the drying and/or detailing process if you offer such extras. The dimensions may vary depending on the layout of your car wash. An experienced car wash architect can help you determine exactly how much space you'll need.

Lose Your Lease, Lose Your Wash

One of the biggest arguments against leasing is that there is always the danger, if you are not careful to negotiate a lease with terms that are favorable to you, that you could lose your wash when your lease expires. Should the owner of the land decide not to renew your lease, you'll be permitted to take all your equipment, but the money you spent constructing the building will be lost. While that's certainly an extreme danger and one serious enough to have caused many owners to absolutely swear off leasing as an option, there are some ways you can insulate yourself against this possibility.

Always Push for Long Lease Terms

Obviously, if you lease your land from year to year as opposed to having a ten-year lease, you're in much greater jeopardy of losing your business at the whim of the landowner or if nothing else, having constant rent increases. If the change is dramatic enough, it could make a once-profitable wash a prime candidate for bankruptcy.

Options to Renew

Another way to protect your business from the whims of the landowner is to negotiate for an option, or options, to renew. Essentially this means that, once your lease is up, you have the option to renew it for a certain period of time at a previously agreed upon rate. For example, if you have an initial lease period of ten years, with two options to renew for seven years each, you have essentially secured your rights to use the land for 24 years (ten years on the initial agreement, plus seven years on the first renewal and seven more on the second renewal). Not only do you know that your building won't be taken away, but you can also determine with relative accuracy what your land costs are going to be.

What Is a Good Lease Price?

The answer to this question depends on several factors. How big is the lot? How many bays or what size car wash can it accommodate? How desirable is the location? In general, what constitutes a fair lease price will be determined by the car wash size, what the land can support, and the location. For example, land that will support a building large enough to accommodate a six-bay, self-service car wash will be worth more than a smaller parcel that will only accommodate a four-bay unit. Using the same logic, land that is perfectly situated in a prime, wash-friendly location is going to be worth more (at least to you) than a similarly sized parcel in a less desirable location. If the land is highly in demand, such as a lot in a major city, it will be much costlier than land in a rural area where there is more available space.

There are no hard and fast rules about what you should pay to lease your land, but here are some guidelines. According to an *Auto Laundry News* survey, rent, on average, was about 15.5 percent of gross revenues for full-service and exterior-conveyor washes. In other words, after you've determined or estimated what you can reasonably expect to make from a car wash built on a particular parcel of land, you should probably try to avoid paying more than about 15.5 percent of that amount to rent the space.

As an example, let's take a look at an exterior-conveyor wash to see how this works. An exterior-conveyor car wash servicing 50,000 cars a year and averaging around

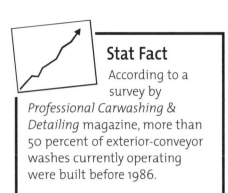

$5.50 in gross revenue a car, will have projected annual revenue of $275,000. To figure out what an acceptable lease agreement would be in order to make this a viable proposition, we first calculate 15.5 percent of $275,000. This comes to $42,625. Now divide that by 12 to determine a fair monthly rate, and you get about $3,552.

Of course, that price may not work economically if you're operating a much smaller business—such as a three-bay, self-service car wash that may only generate around $55,000 in gross annual revenue. In that instance, you're looking for land that will cost in the range of $710 a month to lease.

Use these figures for what they are—guidelines. There are undoubtedly washes that pay more for land and succeed, just as there are undoubtedly washes that pay less than that and fail. But at least by knowing some general numbers, you'll be able to tell if your business is doomed before it ever gets off the ground or if you've stumbled upon a truly sweet deal.

Other Lease Factors

In addition to those provisions we've already mentioned, there are some other things you might want to look for in a lease. One of those might be an option to buy the land outright at some future date, or at least a right-of-first-refusal should the current owner decide to sell. Although it's probably very unlikely that you'll be able to get a purchase option, it's slightly more plausible that an owner will agree to a right-of-first-refusal clause. The value of these and the other provisions (such as an option to renew) is that they protect you should situations change unexpectedly. Because you don't own the land, you should be making every attempt to insulate yourself and your business from a leasing disaster. It might seem like an extra headache, but it's not too far off-base to say that taking the time to investigate these provisions could mean the difference in whether or not you'll still have a car wash business five or ten years from now.

Buying Your Land

While leasing might seem complicated, buying isn't exactly a walk in the park, either. Sure, you don't have to worry that a landlord will suddenly pull the rug out from under

your feet or triple your rent, but buying land requires that you have more capital at your disposal. In some cases, this one factor might make the decision for you.

If you're considering buying the land, it's a good idea to hire a real estate agent who can help you through the process. You might also want to contact car wash experts to evaluate a site before you put down any money. Additionally, a business plan—which you should have in any case—is even more important, because you will likely be seeking investors or a major loan from a financial lender and a business plan is a must when trying to procure such funding. More on business plans at the end of this chapter.

Tip...

Smart Tip

What's the best car wash investment? Some experts say it's a wash that is in a good location but that hasn't been cared for. The price may be below market value and with a little elbow grease, and some good marketing, you can revamp the site and capitalize on the great location.

Insurance Issues

As stated earlier, you can't go into business without insurance. While the amount of insurance will vary depending on the type of car wash you open, there is some basic coverage that you will need. Here are some of the things your insurance policy should cover:

- *Your building and its contents.* Coverage should pay to replace any loss of your car wash and equipment.
- *Loss of business income.* If a disaster happens and you need to close your wash for an extended period of time, you're going to need insurance to recoup your losses.
- *Equipment breakdown.* In addition to insurance coverage that protects you in case your equipment is destroyed, you should also look for coverage in case your equipment simply breaks down.
- *General liability.* This very important insurance protects you against lawsuits, injury claims, damage claims, etc.
- *Workers' compensation.* If you have employees, you need to carry coverage that protects you against injuries to your workers.

You may decide on more coverage, but those are the basics. Your local car wash association may also have some sort of group insurance arrangement as part of its membership benefits, so you might want to look into that possibility, too. You can also check out the Insuracenter in Joplin, Missouri (www.carwashinsurance.com), a company that specializes in insuring car washes.

Beware!
When buying an existing wash, ask to see revenue statements from at least the past three years. Never, ever accept as proof of revenue what the current owner claims are "representative" months. They could be the best months the wash has ever had. Have all information in writing, with documents as backup.

Should You Buy or Build Your Car Wash?

For a novice car wash owner, we'll go out on a limb here and say it's probably going to be easier for you to buy an existing car wash than to build a new one from the ground up. Why? One reason is that an existing business is somewhat of a known entity. You know how much revenue the business takes in every year. You know what the costs of operation are. In addition, customers already know that the business exists. Mark G. bought an existing business, as did Dick H., the car wash owner in Sacramento, California. Entrepreneur Richard K., in Chicago, also bought an existing business, but he did some remodeling to expand and update the car wash.

Buying is also less complicated. There are no architects, no construction plans, no building permits, and (perhaps most important) very little lag time between when you purchase the business and when you actually start operating, unless you plan on doing major renovations.

However, there are also some limitations when trying to buy an existing car wash. For one, it's not always easy to find a seller in the area in which you want to start your business. A significant number stay in business for many years and may then stay in the family, perhaps being turned over from father to son. With price tags of $2 million or more, many new entrepreneurs are finding it may be just as cost effective to buy land and build from scratch rather than waiting for a new car wash to become available and paying the high asking prices. The other argument for buying land and building a car wash is that you get the car wash you want and in a competitive business this can be very important—you don't want to get saddled with an antiquated wash and then have to put another $500,000 into the business to upgrade the equipment. Building a car wash allows you to design the facility to fit the neighborhood, meet the latest in zoning and regulatory issues, and compete in the most effective manner.

If you are planning to buy the land, make sure to do environmental studies and be able to meet all of the necessary criteria and requirements for the town, county, or state before making a purchase. If you are looking to buy an existing car wash, consider using a car wash broker who will be more knowledgeable about buying a facility. Visit www.carwashbrokers.com for some leads.

Regulatory Issues

The licenses and permits you will need to operate your wash are going to vary according to your local laws and regulations. Some car washes need in excess of 15 licenses and/or permits according to Steve Gaudreau. You should be in contact with your local government or chamber of commerce to determine which licenses you will need. They may include licenses or permits that cover water use and/or pollution and environmental concerns. If you plan on constructing extensive signage, you'll have to check local zoning ordinances to find out the size and location of signage that's permitted.

If you add offline services such as oil changes, gas sales, propane sales, a gift shop, or food service, you'll probably need additional permits. You should work with your lawyer, who can help make sure that you are in total compliance with your local government's regulations.

Environmental Concerns

One of the most significant concerns will be that of water and water runoff. For this reason nearly all car wash owners are installing and using reclaim systems that capture a significant amount, in some cases as much as 80 percent of the water used,

---

Slow It Down

Corner lots are usually great locations for just about any type of business, especially if cars have access to your location from two streets. But there is a downside to what would be an otherwise great location. Americans are an impatient bunch, and judging from the way some people drive, there's nothing we hate more than sitting in traffic or waiting at stoplights. Some anxious drivers might see your lot as a convenient shortcut to bypass traffic. This isn't just annoying; it can be dangerous, too. With customers moving around and cars pulling in and out of wash or vacuum bays, all it takes is one careless driver to ram headlong into an unsuspecting customer or car.

When you're setting up your lot, consider adding speed bumps to force cars to slow down. If you're lucky enough to be on a corner, you might also want to think about installing signs that discourage drivers from using your business as a way to avoid normal traffic delays.

Smart Tip

Tip...

It's important to educate your customers in order to dispel some of the common myths about the car washing process. According to the International Carwash Association, nearly half the owners of conveyor washes (including full-service and exterior-conveyor) provide reprints of articles about car washing to their customers and give information about water recycling and environmental benefits.

and run it through a filtering system that cleans it for re-use. In fact, many states and counties are requiring that some form of reclaim system be in use, especially in areas where droughts are more likely to occur.

"Although it's not the public perception, car washes today are actually more environmentally friendly than washing your car in the driveway and having all of the dirty water and detergents just run off into the street," says Steve Gaudreau.

There are a number of additional environmental concerns your local planning department is likely to have regarding your car wash. These could include oil and/or sludge disposal as well as the chemicals that you are using and, in some cases, disposing of. You should consult the local government in your area to ask for information on the regulations regarding water use and recycling. You may be required to install things such as sand traps to filter out any sludge that's mixed in with your water, before it reaches the sewer drain. The more chemical clean up and water reclaim done by your car wash the better the perception will be, and in an age of increasing environmental awareness, you do not want to be on the wrong side of environmental friendliness. One place you might visit, regarding water reclaim systems is CATEC at wwe.catec.com.

To protect your business, you might want to do a Phase I Environmental Study, which should cost around $2,000. This will help determine, before you ever take possession of a car wash, what environmental damage has already been done to the surrounding area. It's kind of like a walk-through you'd do before taking possession of an apartment or house. You don't want to be held responsible for damage that the previous owner may have caused. If you finance the purchase of an existing wash, your lender may require an environmental study. To find a reputable professional who can conduct an environmental study for your business, ask any industry associations you join for referrals.

As a car wash owner, water is something you're going to come to know a lot about. One of the reasons is that the makeup of your water is going to determine, at least to a certain extent, how well you can wash cars. Another reason is that it's going to affect how customers perceive your wash. (We'll explain that one in a minute.) Finally, the government is going to want to know something about your water as well.

Let's start with how the chemistry of your water affects the quality of the service you provide. What you're concerned with here is how soft or hard your water is.

The key thing to remember here is that you want soft water. Depending on where you are doing business, there may be requirements that a water-softening system be used. Some places of the country, like Los Angeles, have car wash owners who refer to their water as liquid rock—meaning it's incredibly hard and requires treatment to make it up to snuff for car wash standards.

Stat Fact
According to a study from the International Carwash Association, nearly 85 percent of consumers agree with the statement: "Having a clean car makes me feel good."

Local pool-supply stores or water-treatment facilities sell kits that allow you to test your water and determine its level of hardness or softness. You can also ask your water company to do an analysis. The level of hardness or softness is measured in something called "grains." Zero grains hardness is the best for our purposes. Anything between zero and five grains, and you might be able to get by without a softening system. Anything more than five, and you're dealing with liquid rock.

Here's why this is so important: Detergents work best at zero grains hardness. In other words, the soap you use, no matter what soap it is, will clean cars better when your water is soft because the soap mixes more efficiently into the water. A second, equally important reason for using soft water is your equipment. Hard water taxes your equipment much more than soft water does, meaning there's more wear and tear, more breakdowns, more repair costs, and ultimately a shorter life span for the lifeblood of your business.

Soft water is also important in how customers perceive your business. It may sound strange. After all, hard water is something you can't see. It looks just like soft water. It doesn't smell any different than soft water, nor does it taste different. So what difference does it make to your customers if your water is hard or soft? In a word, "bubbles." Your customers like to see bubbles and foam when they drive through your wash. It makes them feel good, like there's really something powerful going on to get the dirt and grime off their cars. Soap foams much better when the water isn't hard. Soft water will also allow you to use less soap, because hard water requires more soap be used to achieve the same level of foaminess.

Assuming that you do need to soften your water, you're going to need equipment to do that. These systems will usually consist of two tanks that work together to soften the water. It's going to require some maintenance and monitoring on your part to make the system function properly. The manufacturer of your system, or the distributor who sold it to you, should be able to provide a complete explanation of how it works and what your responsibilities are in keeping it working.

Here are some ground rules to keep in mind. Your system should be big enough to handle the volume of business your wash does. Anyone who's ever tried to take a hot shower in a house filled with people with an undersized water tank will probably tell you to err on the safe side. What this means is that you should get something that's perhaps slightly larger than you think you might need on an average day. Second, owners without the knowledge of how a water softening system works don't realize that their equipment may be "regenerating"—essentially flushing itself out—at the wrong time of day. You want this to occur at a time when your car wash is either closed or, if you're running a 24-hour self-service wash, when it's not busy (maybe something like 2 A.M. or 3 A.M.).

Naming Your Car Wash

We'll talk a bit more about this in Chapter 10, when discussing marketing and public relations, but for now you should start thinking about what you want to name your car wash. You can get creative and start dreaming up names like "Suds Are Us" or "Slick Willie's" if you want. That's fine. But all the experts say that, no matter what you decide on for a name, the words "car wash" need to be in there.

Try coming up with a name that clearly tells people where your car wash is located, or at least the general area. "Parkside Car Wash" or "Center Street Car Wash" are just a couple of examples. Another alternative is to choose a name that represents the service you ideally want to provide—like "Clean and Convenient Car Wash" or "Speedy Car Wash." Yet another consideration is including the type of car wash you have ("Jerry's Full-Service Car Wash" or "Broadway Self-Service Car Wash," for example).

Writing Your Business Plan

A business plan is essentially a blue print for your business. It is written for a couple of reasons. First, you are likely to need financing and a business plan is a key document when trying to get investors interested in backing your business. It is also important to show lending institutions that you have thought out this plan to open a car wash from every angle and have a complete picture of the business you intend to open, including what finances will be needed, how the money will be spent, and what the projected return on the investment will be in one, three, five, and possibly even ten years down the road.

The other primary reason for writing a business plan is for yourself and those involved in building and running the business. It serves as a living, breathing document that can keep you on track, allow you to see your progress, and can often let you see whether there is or is not growth potential over time. You may look at your business plan and decide that everything is going better than schedule, thus allowing you to expand, perhaps by adding a new profit center. Conversely, your numbers may be lagging behind your projections. This might lead you to assess ways of improving the bottom line by making changes.

The Components of a Business Plan

Your business plan will include the following, plus other information as deemed necessary. These are, however the key elements.

1. *A Table of Contents.* Make it easy to follow for your readers.

2. *The Executive Summary.* Although this comes first, it is often written last after you've thought out all of the various areas of our business. It is here where you provide an overall summary in a page, or perhaps two, of your car wash business, including the reasons why you are starting the business—your goals, plans, and objectives for the business, the industry and your place in the market, your target audience, marketing plans, and future expectations. Remember, however, that this is only a summary, which should entice potential investors to read farther. It is the single most important aspect of a business plan, and one that should provide a concise, factual basis for your car wash being a success. Hint: Avoid the hype (i.e., it will be the greatest car wash the city has ever seen).

3. *Industry Analysis.* Researching this part of the business plan is a marvelous way for you to bone up on the industry. It is also the place in which you describe the car wash industry at present and show your overall knowledge of the market in which you are getting involved. You will need to use numerous resources, such as the International Car Wash Association, *Professional Carwashing & Detailing* magazine (and its web site www.carwash.com), *Auto Laundry News*, and other sources to put together a state of the industry page. You will then show where your car wash will fit into the scheme of things and what you will offer that is on the cutting edge of the industry or at least necessary for the area in which you are opening up your wash.

4. *Business or Operational Overivew.* Here, you will provide a comprehensive overview of your plans for the business. How will the business operate? What kind of business structure will you have? What resources will you need? Where will you be located?

   Explain the equipment that will be necessary and how it will be used. That may include a full-service conveyor, self-service bays, a reclaim system, computerized maintenance system, and security devices. Whatever you plan to have at your car wash, discuss how it works, why you have the equipment, and how much it will cost. Essentially, you want to give the details and highlight the selling points of what your business will offer and how it is beneficial (again, not with hype, but with facts).

5. *Products and/or Services.* Here you will give more specifics on what customers can expect. If you offer detailing, include it here and describe the services. Let

the reader know what to expect from start to finish. This also includes the vac-uuming (full service or self service) and the convenience store items, as well as accessories and vending area. Be careful not to use industry lingo. Explain your products and services in easy-to-understand language.

6. *Your Marketing Plan.* The marketing plan is an important aspect of your overall business and one to which you will need to pay strict attention. The best car wash in the state is not worth very much if nobody knows it is there. In this section you need to first describe your target audience. The size of the market will depend on where you are located. Gather as much background information as possible to support your demographic research (why will this audience come to your wash?). Finally, explain your plan for reaching the audience. Are you planning to adver-tise? Will you use direct mail? The internet? Special promotions and coupons? If you have media contacts or know of publicists that will help you spread the word, include that information in this section. Again, the mere process of writing this section will get you motivated to work on this important area.

7. *Competitive Analysis.* This is also a very important part of the business plan. As much as you'd like to "trash" your competitors, you need to take the high road—or have a professional approach. Discuss all of your direct and indirect competition (meaning other car washes as well as places such as gas stations that offer carwashing as a secondary option). Provide information on their busi-nesses, including their prices along with areas in which they do well and areas in which they are lacking. Finally, use the information you have gathered on your competitors to show what you can improve upon and what will bring cus-tomers to you. This is your competitive edge and what separates the successful entrepreneurs from the wannabes.

8. *Operations Plan.* This is how the car wash will work. Once you have explained what equipment you will have on hand and what sets you apart from your com-petition, you need to provide an overview of who will be doing what. Will you have a computerized menu or a greeter at the front informing customers of the services offered? Will one person be handling the convenience shop and col-lecting payment from the car wash customers or will there be separate cashiers? What will you do throughout the day and how will customer service policies be handled? Think about how the actual operation will unfold.

9. *Management Team.* If you are all alone, then this is a brief overview of why you are the man, or woman, for the job. A few paragraphs should do it, recounting your applicable business experiences. No, lenders and investors do not really care about the car wash you ran in your driveway when you were 12 years old. They are interested in seeing a pattern of responsible business successes if they are going to back you in this venture. The same holds true for potential busi-ness partners.

10. *Financial Plan.* Another biggie, this is where you "show them the money," so to speak. Here, you will include all the financial information from starting up the car wash to balance sheets. Use any charts and graphs necessary to show how you will start up the car wash, how expenses will be handled, and how profit will ensue. Let your accountant help you with this part, and try not to exaggerate or get carried away. Inaccurate financial projections are among the primary reasons why many businesses fail. Be cautious, even conservative if necessary, and show estimates of how you will build your car wash into a moneymaking business. Show the profit and loss statement for the next three, five, seven, and perhaps ten years. Break it up into months and then into years to show the progress and growth of the business. Remember to allow for inflation in your expenses and explain how you will adjust. Support your financial section by including a break-even analysis, a balance sheet, and your projected cash flow.

You may also include supporting material at the end of the business plan, including photos of the car wash you plan to purchase or architectural sketches if you are planning to build, along with your resume and any additional financial documents that support the business plan.

Before showing anyone your business plan, review it very carefully and rewrite it (or at least edit it) several times. You want the plan to answer all of the questions anyone could ask about the future of your business. So as to not reinvent the wheel, there are many books available on how to write a business plan, plus web sites such as www.bplan.com, www.sba.gov (Small Business Administration), and www.inc.com, where you will also find business plans. In addition, there is business plan software available with templates to make life easier, such as Palo Alto's Business Plan Pro, among other products on the market.

While your business plan may be more or less elaborate than others, it is important for all businesses to have a written plan to define where the business is going. Once you are done reviewing and proofreading your plan, have it printed on high-quality paper and bound. It can be the most important document in procuring the funding you need and for keeping you on track with your business during the start-up period and beyond.

6

Start-Up
Expenses

Now we're going to give you the solid financial information you'll need to determine the type of wash that's right for you, based on the capital you have available (or at least have access to).

The good thing about the car wash business is that it can accommodate many different types of owners—from someone who wants a small side business to someone who's ready to enter the industry and make it their sole source of income. If you're the side-business type, you can probably get in with a small self-service wash for just over $100,000. If you want the kind of operation that's going to provide you with a nice return on your investment, then you're going to have to come up with about four times that or more.

If you're buying an existing wash, then obviously the start-up expense is going to be the price you pay (or at least the down payment) plus the legal fees and bank fees that go along with it. Trying to tell you what your start-up expenses will be in this case is a little like trying to tell someone how much it costs to buy a house. You can't do it. It depends on the size of the house, the location, the age, and a host of other factors. Car washes are the same way.

With that said, there are certainly ways to tell if you're getting a good deal. Review the discussion on how to determine a rate of return in Chapter 9. This will give you a good indication of whether the rewards you can expect from a particular wash justify the risks.

Another method would be to look at a figure called the gross income multiplier (GIM). A rough estimate of a "good" multiplier might be anywhere from 2.5 to 3.5. What this means is that you can safely pay 2.5 times to 3.5 times the gross annual revenue of a wash and still be getting a decent deal. In other words, if a wash does $150,000 a year in gross revenues, you should expect to pay between $375,000 and $525,000 for the business. Again, this is a rough guideline, but it can prevent you from overpaying for a site or alert you when you may be getting a steal. As mentioned earlier, car wash brokers for existing sites and good land realtors for starting a business from the ground up are recommended for newcomers. Just select someone with good references that you can talk to first.

If you build a new business, the largest costs are going to be for the land, structure, and the equipment itself. Let's start by looking at some sample costs for a few different kinds of washes (see the charts on pages 83-86). In the examples provided, we've assumed that you're either buying an existing business or building a new wash and leasing the land. If you decide to purchase the land instead, your start-up costs would look a bit different.

Where the Money Goes

Your largest expense initially is going to be acquiring land and equipping it with your washing machinery or acquiring an existing business. But running a car wash is like running any other business. There are a host of other little odds and ends that can add up—and quickly. See the Equipment Checklist on pages 66-67 for an idea of what typical equipment expenses look like for both full- and self-service washes.

One of the advantages to buying an existing wash is that you'll probably be buying many of these things (fax machines, phones, computers, etc.) along with it. But let's assume you don't inherit the equipment or that you need to supplement the equipment that you've acquired with an existing business. What will you need?

The list of equipment you're going to need will vary depending on the type of car wash you'll be starting. For example, while the owner of a full-service wash is going to need a cash register, a self-serve owner won't. But you will need a bill changer instead.

Office Equipment and Supplies

To start, let's tackle the items that are pretty much going to be common to all car washes, regardless of their size or the market they serve.

Computer System and Software

Computers in the car wash industry have a wide range of uses. This range can be from basic record keeping to inventory control to automated teller services and touchscreen menus.

Depending on what you're going to be using the computer for—simple record-keeping or database marketing, for example—you may be able to get away with a simple, inexpensive system for around $1,500. However, most car washes today, at least conveyor washes, are using more advanced software programs designed specifically for the car wash industry. Depending on the specs listed on the program (consider which software program you may want to use before buying your computer) you may need a higher-end machine for several hundred, or even a couple thousand, dollars more. Remember, a computer is an important investment in your business, and computer systems today can save you a tremendous amount of time by monitoring your wash from your inventory to the number of cars that pass through in a given day.

What should you look for in a computer system? Here are some minimum requirements you should check for:

- Pentium IV-class processor
- Current version of Microsoft Windows
- 512MB RAM
- 80GB to 120GB hard drive
- CD-ROM drive (32X or faster)
- Broadband connection

A computer meeting these standards should be able to handle anything you, as a car wash owner, will be likely to need. Of course, there are all types of bells and whistles you can get to go along with the basics, the key, however, as stated earlier, is to make sure to check the software you plan to use ahead of time to make sure your computer is up to the specifications.

The modern office not only includes office equipment but also needs to be wired so that you can utilize the computer programs designed for running a car wash and so that you have fast internet capabilities for research, contacting suppliers, or checking in on the business when you are not physically there. You will also want to network computers if you have more than one location. Computer system integration is a growing business, and you will likely find a systems integrator nearby who can help you bring your computer system up to date and enable you to have the necessary cables and connections to maintain an efficient, modern office.

Computer Peripherals

One "extra" you are going to want is a printer. Here, too, it's possible to break the bank on the latest model. In all seriousness, think about what you're going to be using your printer for—printing fliers, signs, employee manuals, memos, etc. The reason you want to think about it is because you have a couple of choices here. The first is to go with the old standby—a black-and-white laser printer. It will print much sharper images than its inkjet counterparts and only cost a bit more (probably less than $1,000 for a basic model). So if you're satisfied living without color, this is probably the way to go.

Car Wash Software

The car wash industry was one of the first to embrace computer technology as far back as the late 1980s. Today, if you are planning a full service or express exterior car wash, you can make life much easier by purchasing any of several computer software packages and accessories.

The latest methods of automating the conveyor car wash are becoming increasingly popular, as they limit the need for labor, which can add up, while maintaining an efficient business. Tunnel controllers, for example, control the actual electrical relays that tell the rinse to go on for three or four seconds and then go off, followed by the wax, and so on, The tunnel controller turns what the computer knows into electrical switches that control the functions in the tunnel so it does not need to be controlled manually. It's essentially the brains of the tunnel. Depending on the features and the length of the tunnel, a tunnel controller can cost from $7,000 for 24 functions to well over $10,000 for a more sophisticated 96-function tunnel controller.

Tunnel control software will need to interface with your other software, and you can get as elaborate as you deem necessary. Incorporating the more sophisticated TunnelWatch system with point-of-sale system from a company like DRB could run you from $20,000 to $100,000, but make your entire wash run a single high-tech entity, thus eliminating almost all labor and allowing you to enter the high tech "express" world of car washing.

Several point-of-sale systems have also become very popular with car wash owners. One key component is the express pay terminal, where customers can select what type of wash they want and process the payment all from the window of their vehicle. This also allows the option of what DBA calls "Fast Pass," which is really like the Easy Pass sticker that goes in the windshield of a car and identifies that tag and processes that car. It can work in a variety of ways. The system can recognize an unlimited car wash club member or recognize a preferred customer and discount their wash. It can display a separate menu based on their membership status. The direction taken really depends upon the operator and what you want to do with your wash.

Another popular offering is the portable touchscreen terminal held by a greeter or salesperson who greets customers at the entrance of the wash. A system such as SiteWash software can handle credit card acceptance, so it can be an order entry station that allows the customer to pay the greeter from his or her vehicle. Another option is to have it print out a ticket on specifically what the customer wants. Then he or she will take it to the cashier, passing through other point-of-sales areas (such as a mini-convenience store or gift items). According to Ken Brott of DRB Systems Inc., "Many owners like that it creates a more personal customer-friendly atmosphere, where someone is with the customer for entire transaction. It also allows the greeter to make more recommendations and sales." Other touch systems, not unlike those at MacDonald's and other fast food places, allow cashiers to ring up specific items on the system.

You can also buy a car wash software system that features an automatic recharge module, like a health club, where you keep the name of the customer and information on an electronic file. Customers come as often as they like, and their credit card is automatically charged each month. It will show you, as the car wash operator, the usage of the membership pass and how often they're redeeming it so you can make sure you're pricing it right. Data is important, and the most of the latest software informs owners how many cars are passing through the wash on a daily basis and what customers are asking for, in terms of your offered services.

For most car wash owners, it is a matter of selecting the software components that are best for their wash. Some owners feel that speed is of the essence and that getting customers through with a fully operational electronic (computerized) system is the key to success while others find that the lack of personal service loses customers and the greeter with a handheld touchpad menu of options is a big plus.

▲

Software to consider includes:

- *Tunnel Master for Windows* car wash management system. The new *Tunnel Master for Windows* Version 4.0 offers the car wash operator a powerful car wash management, point-of-sale, and controller system. Tunnel Master also features the power of the Intel™ Pentium processor, ensuring speed and reliability. Also check out Tunnel Master Jr. Both are made by Innovative Control Systems. http://www.washnet.com.

- *The Auto Sentry® eXP* is an express pay station that displays touch screens, giving customers an easy-to-understand and use interface. The screen below prompts the user to "Select an Option" to Begin. Made by Innovative Control Systems. http://www.washnet.com.

- *SiteWatch* for Car Wash is a powerful and flexible Windows XP-based POS management system. With SiteWatch, you can run a quick lube, car wash, and other profit centers on a single computer system. SiteWatch lets you collect and transfer sales, labor, and customer history data through your company. It also allows you to customize your point-of-sale system. Made by DRB Systems Inc. www.drbsystems.com.

- *TunnelWatch* for Car Wash works in terms of inches, which results in lower chemical and utility costs, because equipment is activated only when needed, rather than cycling up early or remaining on after a vehicle has passed. A flexible system with a variety of features, TunnelWatch includes anti-collision and pacing. Made by DRB Systems Inc. www.drbsystems.com.

- *The WashSoft®* point-of-sale system is a complete, powerful tool with real-time sales functions that let your ticket writer use vehicle ID data to greet customers by name. You can also capture customer information, sell services, and process loyalty cards through the built-in barcode scanner. The Wash Handheld instantly transfers tickets and real-time information to the cashier and tunnel. Made by Integrated Services Inc. www.ints.com.

- *I Cashier* is equipped with a number of standard security features, including a built-in heavy-duty, patented combination-locked vault and door open sensor that automatically e-mails the wash owner when the door is opened. This system can help build loyalty through a Wash Access Loyalty System (WALS) whereby you can manage loyalty programs over the internet. You can also process transactions quickly and have complete control in accordance with the WashSoft technology.

Basic Office Software

For an in-bay or to run your self-service business, you can start with more simplified software. To start, it's a good idea to just stick with the essentials. You're going to need an accounting program, such as Microsoft Money or Intuit QuickBooks ($80 to

$250); a basic word processing program, such as Microsoft Word or Corel WordPerfect ($85 to $250); and perhaps some type of desktop publishing program. You don't need to go overboard with that last one (some professional packages can cost up to $1,000). You simply need something that will allow you to print fliers or other simple signs.

If you're planning to compile a mailing list, you're going to need software to handle that, too. Microsoft Office (about $500) integrates several programs in one easy package: Word, for word processing; Excel, for creating spreadsheets; PowerPoint, for graphical presentations; and Publisher, for creating simple fliers, cards, brochures, etc. This may be a good option for you because it includes tools that allow you to maintain mailing lists and merge your names with mailings you can compose right on Microsoft Word software.

Phone System

You're going to be on the phone quite regularly between ordering supplies, calling maintenance crews, and staffing your shifts, so you're going to need a decent system. On the other hand, you aren't in the business of telemarketing, so breaking the bank isn't going to be necessary.

Depending on the size of your car wash, you're probably going to want at least two lines. If you opt for a fax machine, figure on three lines. Phone line installation will run you in the neighborhood of $50 to $80 a line. Plan on spending in the range of $80 to $180 for a two-line speakerphone with auto-redial, memory dial, mute button, and other goodies. You're also going to want to have your cell phone handy at all times. Hint: use the cell phone wisely so as not to run up ridiculous monthly bills.

Remember to get an answering machine ($35 to $65 for a basic model; $125 to $200 for one with advanced features). The goal here is simply to make sure that you can be reached whenever you're needed, and that you can reach your employees, your vendors, and your customers. Whatever it takes to accomplish that will do the trick, even if you don't opt for a system with all the bells and whistles the gadget-freak inside of you is longing for.

Miscellaneous Office Equipment

Along with your computer and printer, you may want to add a fax machine, or you can buy an all-in-one printer. In addition, you'll want to have a calculator handy and if you don't have more elaborate software and touch screen technology to handle your casher needs, then you'll want a quality cash register (unless you run a self-serve car wash, in which case you can forget about the cash register). You may also want to invest in equipment, such as a paper shredder (yes, people will go through your garbage looking for goodies such as Social Security numbers or bank account statements) and a photocopier. All of these can be purchased at your typical office

Equipment Checklist

Here are the equipment and supplies that you'll need or want to have.

We've provided a high-end estimate for a full-service car wash and low-end estimate for a self-service car wash with two wash bays. Both scenarios assume that you are building a new business and will need to acquire equipment.

Keep in mind that your equipment costs will vary depending on whether you decide to buy an existing wash (which should come with much of the equipment you'll need) or build from scratch (in which case you'll need to buy the equipment you need to get started). And remember, it is possible to build a car wash without some of the equipment listed below. These costs are general guidelines for what you can expect to pay.

Equipment	Full-Service	Self-Service
Wash-Related Equipment		
Full power-wash equipment	$350,000	$ 0
Self-Serve equipment	0	(2 bays) 40,000
Vacuums	(10 units) 6,000	(2 units) 2,000
Automatic dryers	(1 unit) 23,000	0
Water heater	17,000	8,000
Water reclamation/recycling	30,000	15,000
Water softener	7,000	7,000
Retail/Lot Equipment		
Shaded vacuum area	4,500	0
		(continued on page 67)

supply store, such as Office Depot or Staples. Browse the catalog or go online. Stay within your budget without sacrificing quality.

Office Furniture

Again, this cost will vary depending on the type of car wash you own. If you own a self-serve, there's probably a better than even chance that your office will be located off-site, perhaps even in your home, and you may be able to get away with using what you already have. If, however, you're equipping an office at your wash, there are a few things you're going to need.

Equipment Checklist, continued

Equipment	Full-Service	Self-Service
Retail/Lot Equipment		
Floor heater	$8,500	(2 bays) $4,000
Vending machines	(1 unit) 2,500	0 (free from a distributor such as Coke or Pepsi)
Car wash-specific computer software	50,000	0
Change machines	1,500	(2 units) 1,550
Signage	12,000	1,500
Security system	5,000	500
Landscaping	500	200
Trash receptacles	500	50
Bathroom fixtures	750	0 (assuming you don't provide facilities)
Cash register	3,000	0
Lighting	2,500	(exterior) 1,000
Inventory	10,000	800
Office equipment	10,000	2,000
Total	**$544,250**	**$83,600**

Most car wash owners would never think about being elaborate with their office space, assuming that they even have office space that's not a spare bedroom or den. That's one of the nice things about this business—you're certainly not going to spend the majority of your time being a paper pusher. Figure on a desk, chair, and filing cabinet as the main expenses in equipping your office. You can probably get by spending less than $400 for these items. Then throw in miscellaneous office supplies such as paper, fax cartridges, CDs, folders, staples, paper clips, and what have you, and you're still talking less than $500, if you spend wisely. Not bad. (That's probably just about all you'll be able to afford anyway after the real equipment—your washing equipment—is taken care of.)

Wash-Related Equipment

Of all the decisions you make in starting your new wash, this is going to be one of the most important. The supplier you choose and the equipment you buy will probably impact your business for the next 15 to 20 years. It will also be a factor in the price of your wash if you decide to sell it at some point down the road.

With a decision this monumental, you'd probably like us to give you some definite answers about exactly which systems to buy and which manufacturer to use. Most manufacturers today produce quality equipment, and the one you choose to go with will probably have less of an impact on your business than one other very important factor—your local distributor.

Why is this so important? The manufacturer is typically not the one you're going to call if you have a problem that needs fixing ASAP. You're usually going to call the person who actually sold, delivered, and installed your system. If that person is unreliable or is located two hours away, you're going to have problems.

Establishing a Relationship with Your Distributor

Your decision on which equipment to buy should basically be driven by how you feel about working with the various distributors. If you're choosing between two different pieces of equipment, both of which are suitable for the services you want to provide, go with the better distributor (assuming the prices are comparable).

When we say "better distributor," that might mean different things to different people. So here are some specific things you should look for:

- *The distributor is located close by.* Generally, you're going to want to stay away from a distributor that is located in an area that's going to make it difficult for him to get to you quickly and easily if there's a problem. Some owners have chosen specific distributors simply because their offices were close by, while a competitor's was a couple of hours away, even though that second distributor's equipment was a tad better.

- *The distributor has been in business for a long time.* It's pretty hard to stay in business for any length of time if you're not good at what you do. Some distributors are family-owned businesses, passed down from generation to generation, indicating that they have a record of satisfying customers and that they aren't planning to go out of business any time soon. We're not saying that new distributors should be dismissed out of hand, but you certainly can't beat the comfort level that comes with a long track record.

- *The distributor provides references.* There's a fairly obvious element to this: A distributor with a long list of references to provide is more desirable than one who, for one reason or another, can't provide you with the names of any of his customers. You want to ask for references so that you can see what type of experience a prospective distributor has, as well as his track record for serving customers. Not so obvious is that a distributor should, if you ask, be willing to tell you the truth about customers who haven't been happy. Anyone who has been in business for any length

> **Bright Idea**
>
> Need help convincing politicians or customers that your wash is environmentally friendly? Tell them about a book called *50 Simple Ways to Save the Earth* (published for the first Earth Day). The authors say that a self-service car wash is the most water-efficient way to wash a car.

of time is going to have had at least one customer who was unsatisfied. If the distributor is candid with you about an account they lost or a customer who was unhappy, it may provide insight into whether he is the best distributor for the type of car wash you plan to open.

- *The distributor knows your type of business.* It can help if the person you're dealing with has experience working with the type of car wash you plan to operate. For example, if the only car washes a prospective distributor has ever worked with are self-serves, he may not be the best choice if you have your sights set on a full-service wash.

New vs. Used Equipment

Car wash equipment isn't cheap, so we should probably spend some time talking about how to make good buying decisions. Properly cared for, your wash-related equipment should last a very long time (perhaps 20 years or so), but it's still a major investment.

Some new owners like the idea of buying used equipment as a way to cut their start-up costs. This can be a cost savings, or it can come back to haunt you. By all means, if you can find quality equipment that has been well maintained and is relatively new, you certainly could save yourself a bundle by outfitting your new wash with at least some used equipment. If you're thinking about going this route, consider the factors listed below carefully:

- *Service.* Will you have someone you can call if the equipment breaks down? When you buy new equipment, you're also getting a distributor who services it. When you buy used equipment, you might not. In the long run, if you have to pay extra to have the equipment serviced, it may turn out that it actually becomes more expensive to buy used equipment.

- *Maintenance.* As with any piece of machinery, car wash equipment will last longer when it's properly maintained. Before making any kind of investment in used equipment, you should ask to see the maintenance records. What you're looking for is basically the same kind of stuff you'd be looking for if you were buying a used car. Was the machinery "tuned up" regularly? Have any parts been replaced recently? Pay special attention to parts that seem to have a tendency to wear out frequently. If a particular bearing or some other part has been replaced more than normal wear and tear would warrant, it could be that there's a larger problem. In other words, you may be getting a lemon. Also look to see if any parts might need to be replaced soon. You wouldn't want to buy a car that was going to need a new clutch in 1,000 miles—at least not at the price the owner is asking. It's basically the same thing with car wash equipment.

- *Water quality.* In Chapter 5, where we discussed testing your water for hardness, we mentioned that hard water tends to make equipment wear out a bit faster than if the water is soft. You might want to ask the current owner about the conditions under which the machinery was used. Ask specifically what the level of water hardness (how many grains of hardness) was under typical operating conditions. If it was anything more than four, you may be buying a piece of equipment that will have a shorter than average service life.

- *Reasons the current owner is selling.* This should be an obvious question. You want to know why the current owner sees the need to get rid of used equipment. Did he just buy brand-new equipment as part of a major renovation or overhaul? Or does his new equipment look pretty much the same as what he's trying to sell you? If it's the latter, you might suspect there's some specific problem with this equipment. Is he going out of business? This is probably a good sign (for you, that is, not him). If the current owner is selling off his equipment because he no longer needs it, it's certainly a better sign than an owner who clearly could use the equipment but is trying to unload it.

What Do You Need?

Let's take a look at the wash-related equipment you'll need for the type of car wash you plan to open.

Self-Service Equipment

A self-service car wash is going to be the easiest and least expensive wash to equip. The two most basic pieces of equipment that you are going to need are a pumping station and a wash module that dispenses the hot, soapy water for washing and clean water for a rinse cycle. The wash module system will typically include a coin meter with a timer, trigger spray wand with swivel, nozzle, gun hose and wand holder, plus foaming brushes. High pressure lines will run from the pumps to the ceiling booms. These are just some of the parts of each bay, plus bay instruction signs so that customers know how to operate the system. You can add your own rules and regulations, but operating instructions typically come with the equipment.

There are other options you can add, such as special cycles that can make your self-service what might be considered "high end." The options include a presoak, tire-cleaning, engine-cleaning, or wax-dispensing cycle—all options that your customers might find appealing. To clean their cars, customers will put money or tokens into your machine, which will activate the cleaning "wand" (where all of this stuff comes out). This, of course, means you're going to need a bill changer on the premises to allow people to get the tokens they're going to need to activate the machinery.

Beware!

Before committing to any kind of vendor, do a search on the internet for "business background checks." This will take you to a number of sites where you can find information on the legal history of a company you're thinking about purchasing from. If you find negative information, like a plethora of lawsuits, you'll probably want to avoid doing business with them.

You may be asking why what seems like an inexpensive setup costs so much. Well, because a self-service car wash is a lot like an iceberg—what the customer actually sees is really only a small part of all the equipment that makes it work. To start, the dispenser isn't just a hose with a brush attached to it; it's a sophisticated high-pressure, water-dispensing system. It also has the ability to mix soap with the water in very precise amounts to give the best cleaning capability. If you have an option that allows customers to apply wax, it has to have the ability to do that as well.

Unless you expect your water to heat itself, you're going to need a fairly substantial water heater. How large will depend on a whole bunch of factors, including the number of bays you have, how many customers you serve, and the style of your equipment. Your supplier will be able to recommend the correct size for your particular situation.

Depending on where you are located, you will probably also need a system to soften your water (these run in the range of $4,000 to $5,000 for a basic system) and a "weep" system. A weep is something that allows for a continuous flow of water through your equipment and helps prevent frozen wands and pipes when the temperature dips below freezing. Wands either come equipped with a weep system or not, so be sure to ask your distributor before you buy.

Dollar Stretcher

Water reclamation systems don't only cut down on your water bill, they can also reduce your water-heating expenses by as much as 50 percent. Plus, they can reduce your soap usage by 35 to 50 percent, according to the folks at www.washguys.com.

Nearly all car washes today are required to have some type of water reclaim system. What these systems do is to essentially recycle the water so that you aren't dumping thousands of gallons of water into the sewer system. Even if you aren't required to have one, you may want to look into it anyway. These systems can save tremendous amounts of water. Basically, the only time exclusively fresh water is used when you operate with one of these systems is during the wash cycle. The cost of the system (approximately $15,000 for a basic system) may very well be offset by the money you'll save on your water bills.

You're also going to need some type of floor heater to help get rid of ice that may accumulate on the floors of your bays during cold periods (cost range $3,000 to $5,000). People can't wash cars in the dark, so you're also going to need some sort of lighting system, especially if you plan on leaving your wash open at night or 24 hours a day (see the "Lighting" section on page 79).

In terms of your absolutely essential equipment, that's pretty much it. There are a whole host of other things you might want to invest in, and we'll get to those in a second. But first, we're going to give you some ideas about how to set up one of the most important sections of your car wash—the equipment room. This is where the rest of that iceberg resides. It's easy to ignore this and not put much thought into what it's going to look like. After all, it's the bays your customers will see, not the equipment room. Despite this, spend a little bit of time thinking about the layout of the room, because it's a lot easier (and cheaper) to get things done right the first time. When setting up this space and laying out the facility, you may want to consult with the Car Wash College in Florida, talk to a consultant, or contact the International Car Wash Association for recommendations. If you're buying an existing wash, you can still take the time now to change things around a bit if they aren't to your liking.

Your change machine is vitally important. In essence, this is your on-the-spot bank. Whatever money is in that change machine represents all the money you've made since the last time you emptied it. If you pick up your money once a day, and thieves steal a day's worth of revenue, that's 14 percent of your weekly revenue gone. Try to locate the machine in an area that's very visible. If you put it behind a wall or some other obstruction, thieves will have a much easier time breaking into it—and your customers will have a hard time finding it. You may also want to think about getting two change machines. The reason is that if one breaks down, you'll still have one in working order. If people can't get access to change or tokens to operate your wash, you might as well not even be open.

Stat Fact

According to a recent report by the International Carwash Association, 86 percent of self-service owners say vacuums are the most popular extra service they offer. For conveyor washes, whether full-service or exterior-conveyor only, wax is the most popular add-on.

Now let's get to a couple of the other options we were talking about. Basically, these will consist of vacuuming facilities and vending machines. These may seem like small potatoes compared to the actual car washing service itself, but that's not really true. These non-essential services can dramatically boost your bottom line.

Let's talk about vending machines first. You can sell pretty much anything you can think of in these machines, from soft drinks and snacks to air fresheners

> **Bright Idea**
>
> Think about what extra bells and whistles you can provide that will make your car wash a more pleasant experience. One owner has a regular customer who routinely runs his car through his automatic bay two or three times in a single visit simply because he likes the color bubbles the soap creates! He says they relax him.

and condoms. You may want to be a bit careful about the kinds of things you sell. As one owner puts it, "Don't sell anything in your machines you won't mind cleaning up off the floor." But you don't want to rule anything out simply because it's not your standard vending-machine fare.

Vacuum islands are another way to capture more revenue for each car. The number of vacuum islands you install is up to you, but you want to try to strike a balance between making sure that the facilities are easy for your customers to use (i.e., there aren't ten cars stacked up in line waiting for them to get free) and not

Leading Equipment Makers and Distributors

While it's one thing to read about all of the possible equipment (and there are numerous options available), it's another to see what we're talking about. These are some of the major equipment makers and distributors that you'll want to visit online. Here, you'll get to see the various pieces of car wash equipment that you can choose from.

- ❍ AOK Equipment at www.aokequipment.com
- ❍ D&S Car Wash Systems at www.dscarwash.com
- ❍ Fuller's Carwash Equipment Co. at www.fullerscwe.com
- ❍ Grant Sales at www.grantsales.com
- ❍ Hanna Car Wash Systems at hannacarwash.com
- ❍ Mark VII Equipment at www.markvii.net
- ❍ Ohio Car Wash Supply Company at www.ohiocarwashsupply.com

▲

having them sit idle. One island for every two bays might be a reasonable place to start, because you can always install more islands at a later date if you find that they're a popular option.

Another option you have is to create an entirely new type of bay—one that isn't self-service at all. This would be a bay that houses automatic washing equipment. This is really a distinct type of wash all its own, so we'll devote an entire section to it next.

In-Bay Automatic Equipment

An in-bay automatic car wash is sort of a compromise between a self-service and an exterior-conveyor wash. This equipment is usually housed in a bay similar to one that you'd find at a self-service wash, except it's bigger. It's also more expensive to equip (about $30,000 to $40,000, or two to three times the cost of equipping a single

---

Automatically Speaking

If your new car wash business is going to be primarily a self-service operation, you still may want to consider installing an in-bay automatic unit as a supplement. There are some compelling reasons for doing this. For example, an in-bay with an automatic rollover unit installed will often be more profitable than a self-service bay. An automatic could pull in 300 percent more revenue than a self-service bay alone. One owner we interviewed, Richard K., who has operated a self-service wash in the Chicago suburbs for 17 years, wishes he had more than the one in-bay automatic unit he has now. The reason? It makes him more money per unit than his bread-and-butter self-service bays.

Another compelling reason to consider adding an in-bay automatic unit is that you have the potential to significantly expand your customer base. As we've stated before, there are basically four types of car washers: the home washer, the do-it-yourself washer who patronizes self-service washes, the exterior-only washer who visits either exterior-conveyor washes or in-bay automatic washes, and the full-service customer. When you can combine two of these market segments, especially at the "low-rent" end of the spectrum, you've effectively captured about 50 percent of the car wash market. Customers who might normally have driven past your wash on their way to the exterior conveyor down the street, might reconsider if they can get an in-bay automatic wash from you—especially if it's more convenient for them or if it can provide a wash that's close in quality but will generally cost less.

---

self-service bay). You may also need to lease more space or buy more land to accommodate the new equipment, which is larger than your typical standard self-serve bay. Those are the downsides—larger space requirements and a bigger investment in terms of capital. It's also probably going to be a bit harder to maintain, because there are simply more moving, automated parts. Furthermore, installing an in-bay automatic unit really creates a domino effect throughout the rest of your facility. For example, you'll probably have to install a larger water heater and pump system to keep up with the demands of the automatic equipment. (Your distributor will be able to help you determine exactly what you need to do to have everything functioning properly.) This cost is in addition to the cost of the equipment. The upside is that you can generally expect more revenue from an in-bay automatic wash, and it's still a self-serve inasmuch as you may not need an attendant present all the time.

At an in-bay automatic rollover, the customer pays at entry, using a similar payment system to the self-serve bays, then drives the car into the wash bay where the rollover system applies chemicals, water, and rinses. There are some rollover systems that are touch free (not touching the vehicle) and others that use brushes and foam action while literally rolling over the car. That's the basic setup. You can also opt for extras such as a wax cycle, an undercoating cycle, and a wheel cleaner, as

Beware!

Think there's no need to post instructions around your equipment? One owner who was having trouble with his equipment opened the coin box to find a dollar bill folded up in the size of a quarter and stuffed through the slot. It's an amusing story, but if the owner hadn't discovered it right away, that bay would have been out of operation for hours. Additionally, you need to remember that we are living in a litigious society, meaning if someone does something wrong, they'll blame you for not instructing them on how to do it correctly and even sue you. Heck, a student "mooning" a friend fell out of his dorm room window and then sued the school for not posting a sign of the dangers of falling out a window—it's true! The more signs, warnings, and instructions you post, the less you can be held liable for the actions of the customer and any mistakes he or she makes.

well as a dryer—all of which will add to the price of the unit. However, these options can pay for themselves with the extra revenue they'll generate. A good rollover in-bay system can usually accommodate 10 to 15 cars per hour.

There is a note of caution about automatic rollover equipment. They have a bit of a "spotty" reputation (no pun intended) for their ability to do a thorough job of cleaning. Think of it this way: With a self-service wash, the customer is controlling how long the cycle is and can physically inspect the car before finishing up to make sure everything is clean. With an exterior conveyor, the equipment is more powerful, and there's usually someone to either prep the car for a better wash or to inspect it at the end of the cycle to make sure everything worked properly. With an in-bay automatic wash, you don't have any of these quality control safeguards.

Nevertheless, many self-service owners do opt to add at least one in-bay automatic unit as part of their package. They do this for a couple of reasons. First, it can help capture some of those customers who simply won't use self-service equipment. Second, as we said before, they can often generate more revenue than by having self-service bays alone. From what we've seen, if you want to go ahead and spend the extra money to install an in-bay automatic unit as part of an existing self-service wash, it's probably not a bad idea. But if you expect an in-bay automatic wash to be your sole source of revenue, you might want to think twice. Why? You'll see them at convenience stores or gas stations—in other words, places that aren't necessarily treating the car washing service as their main source of revenue. There might simply be too much competition in your area for an in-bay automatic wash only. You may be able to beat (or at least coexist) with your competition by offering self-service equipment and an in-bay automatic unit. Remember, self-service and in-bay automatic patrons are two different kinds of customers. But with an in-bay automatic wash alone, you may not be able to beat the gas station a couple blocks away with an automatic rollover wash that costs about half of what you charge—and offers the opportunity for customers to get gas at the same time.

Exterior-Conveyor and Full-Service Equipment

This is the big daddy of equipment start-up costs. Equipping a site with an exterior-conveyor tunnel can cost you in the range of $150,000 to $500,000. You can buy various tunnel sizes depending on the restrictions imposed by the size of your lot. The tunnels themselves will generally vary in length ranging from 70 feet to 120 feet. Most exterior-conveyor washes do basically the same thing—dispense soap, wash the car, rinse the car, apply wax or a rust-inhibiting undercoat, and dry the car—though there are variations.

Just as you can buy any one of a number of cars that will get you from place to place, there are distinct differences in how they are made and what they offer. The same holds true when buying a conveyor car wash system for a full serve or express conveyor car wash.

You will see that a number of the major manufacturers offer similar equipment, with various differences in the details and the features. This is another place where you may want to ask a consultant or do some reading on the manufacturer's web site about the intricacies of each system so that you can make an informed decision.

The machinery in a conveyor car wash is designed to move the car through different stages of the wash cycle while applying high-pressure foam, water, soap sprays, and brushes to clean every corner of the car. This may include complex systems that wash under the chassis, the tires, hubcaps, and almost every part of the car. There is typically a drier system at the end. There are a variety of soft touch, soft brushes, rinses, touch free accessories, and vacuum systems that may also be included.

Of course, to support the conveyor system, you'll have hydraulic power packs, water reclaim systems, air compressors, high- and low-pressure pump stations, and hot water heaters, all supported by a strong source of power and managed by computer systems to make sure everything is working properly. Clearly, anyone planning to build a conveyor car wash will need to review the various equipment in greater detail. For those buying an existing system, you will want to know exactly what model system is installed, when it was installed, and who services it. From that point you can determine whether it is time to make some changes by adding on some new equipment or whether it may be time to do a complete equipment overhaul, which is expensive, but may be necessary if the equipment is antiquated. Look this over carefully before purchasing an existing tunnel, because equipment is the lifeblood of the conveyor wash, whether it is full service or express.

The difference between a full-service and express-conveyor really has very little to do with equipment, but rather with the extra services the owner provides, i.e., vacuuming, glass cleaning, interior cleaning, etc. If you're planning on providing a full-service wash, you can decide whether or not to install vacuuming stations on your lot. It's probably a good idea to do so if you plan to offer an exterior-only cleaning package so that you can allow your customers to do the interior part themselves. If you're going to be exclusively an exterior wash, then vacuum services are going to be almost essential. Plan on spending about $1,000 for each vacuum unit.

Of course, you'll also need the other standard equipment that we discussed for self-service and in-bay automatic washes, such as a water heater, water softener system, and water reclamation system. This will cost you the most for a conveyor car wash as indicated in the pricing earlier.

Retail/Lot Equipment

Generally speaking, unless you have an additional $500,000 to spend, if you're buying an existing car wash, there probably isn't that much that you can do about the existing infrastructure of the business (i.e., building size and construction, machinery and equipment placement, etc.). Much of your investment is already in the existing equipment, so (again) look it over carefully.

There are some areas that you can change, including landscaping, lighting, signage, and similar items. If you're building from scratch, of course, everything is in your power to decide—within the confines of your space and budget.

▲

To Shade or Not to Shade

If you're providing customers with facilities to vacuum or detail their own cars after they've gone through your wash, one of the decisions you're going to have to make is whether to provide shade for your customers. This isn't just a question of being a nice guy and wanting your customers to be comfortable. It's a matter of dollars and cents. Customers probably aren't going to want to use your vacuums if they have to stand in the hot sun on a scorching day to do it. On the other side of the coin, if it's frigid, they might welcome the sun's warmth. What should you do? First of all, consider the climate and determine which will be more beneficial most of the time. The cost for an area that can accommodate three cars at once (about 18 by 27 feet) is around $3,500.

Security

Security is a major concern for today's car wash owners. We're not saying there's a nationwide crime spree occurring at our country's car washes, but there have been several high profile cases of major crimes, such as murder, being committed against car wash customers. These kinds of incidents are unfortunate for an industry already struggling with a bad reputation. It's easy to see why getting a reputation for being unsafe will severely cripple your new wash. For this reason, you should give some serious consideration to how you'll make your wash as safe as you can for your customers. You're also going to need to concentrate on how to make your wash as safe as you can for you and your employees. Let's focus on some steps you can take to increase safety on your premises.

A good security system will accomplish three things: It will safeguard your customers, it will safeguard you and your employees, and it will safeguard your money.

Covering Up

If you own a self-service car wash, it probably won't be very long before you start searching for the best way to cover the walls of your wash bays. Here's a tip: Some owners say fiberglass wallboards are the way to go. They're more attractive than exposed brick and are easier to clean, too. One thing you're probably going to want to avoid is paint. For one thing, the kind of paint you'll have to buy is very expensive. Plus, it tends to deteriorate after only a year or two, meaning you're either going to have to repaint frequently or put up with a wash that looks run-down.

Exactly what kind of system you install is going to be dependent on a number of factors. You can ask the previous owner what worked for him if you're buying an existing wash, or the architect or supplier if you're building a wash from scratch. Price should be a factor in your decision, but remember, just one crime at your car wash can cost you lots of money in lost goods and lost customers. A simple security camera might cost only several hundred dollars, while an elaborate networked surveillance system could run you several thousand dollars. A cheap alternative, one that should cost less than $100, would be to buy fake security cameras and position them at highly visible points around your wash. Sometimes just the threat of being taped might be enough to deter crime. However, this can be a big risk.

You also need to buy secure doors to close a conveyor wash at night. Discuss with manufacturers, like Mark VII, the various possibilities for secure doors and then make sure to have some type of alarm system installed.

Lighting

There's more to creating a safe environment than just installing the latest high-tech equipment to deter criminals. It should also be your goal to create the perception in people's minds that they'll be safe pulling into your wash, getting out of their cars, and using your services. You can accomplish this in several ways.

How and where you choose to install exterior lights is an important consideration, especially for unmanned car washes, such as self-service washes that are operational 24 hours a day. You need adequate lighting in the bays themselves, as well as in the surrounding lot areas. You don't want your bays to be an oasis of light while the rest of your property remains a desert of darkness. Exactly what you'll be able to do in terms of outdoor lighting may be limited by local ordinances. On the flip side, local laws or regulations may require extensive lighting. Whichever side of the coin your municipality falls on, it's always safer to err on the side of caution—if you're unsure as

All about Garbage

Some owners have problems with trash cans blowing over in strong winds or having them kicked over by vandals. Want a simple solution? Try contacting a local concrete company to help you out with a concrete receptacle that's similar to those you see on some city streets and outside fast-food restaurants. Because they're extremely heavy, there's very little chance anyone will be able to tip them over, or worse yet, steal them.

to whether you need extra lighting somewhere on your lot, it's probably best to go ahead and install something.

In the bays themselves, you're going to want to strike a balance between providing enough lighting to allow your customers to feel safe and do a good job washing their cars while not blinding them with light so bright that it becomes uncomfortable. This may sound like a trivial matter, but you'd be surprised at the debate many self-service owners have about what wattage and type of bulbs to use in their bays. There doesn't seem to be one solution that works for everyone, but bulbs that are 250 watts are a pretty common choice, so you might want to start there and make adjustments if need be. Lighting may cost you anywhere from $1,000 to $3,000, depending on the size of your car wash.

Signage

There's a quite lengthy discussion of signage in the marketing chapter (Chapter 10), so we'll only touch on this subject briefly here. Simply put, well thought out signage will help a business draw more customers and easily pay for itself while bringing in additional money. Your exterior signs should be as big as you can possibly make them, as governed by zoning ordinances. People need to see your sign before they think about stopping at your business, and they also need to know at a glance what you're offering. For that reason, the words "car wash" must be the most prominent thing potential customers see. The sign needs to be easily viewed from various angles and cut through the other elements around it. Therefore, the graphics, colors, print, and background all have to be in sync so that the sign catches the driver's eye and makes it clear that he or she is approaching a car wash—and exactly where to turn into the wash.

Interior signage should serve to explain procedures if you have areas of your wash that are left unattended, such as self-serve bays, automatic bays, or vacuum islands. They should also make it easy for a customer to reach someone if there's a problem, clearly explain the pricing system, and say what the customers will get for their money. Again, the print and background need to be very clear so that there is no ambiguity. If prices do not include tax, that needs to be clearly stated as well.

If you need to construct a sign from scratch, it can get pretty expensive—anywhere from $5,000 to $10,000 for both a sign with your business name and something that holds your menu board. Interior signage is much more reasonable and should only run you a few hundred dollars. Do not skimp on signage. As stated earlier, anything that needs to be explained should have a sign, thus eliminating a lawsuit from some misuse of the equipment, such as the woman who used a vacuum to clean her dress and it pulled the dress right off of her.

Landscaping

Without overstating its importance, landscaping is a fairly essential part of most car washes. With that said, you should realize that a beautifully landscaped lot is no substitute for a competitive price and superior service. In fact, some new owners get into trouble by thinking that they'll be able to charge well above the average price in their area simply because their wash is the most attractive. While that's not true, what is true is that proper landscaping can certainly make a difference in the way your wash is perceived in customers' eyes. In addition, many areas require a certain amount of green space on the property for environmental reasons. Therefore, if you need to have some green area, why not make it as aesthetically pleasing as possible.

You don't have to go overboard and hire professional gardeners to outfit your lot with lots of expensive shrubbery, but give some thought to designing something that is both practical (i.e., easy to maintain and doesn't interfere with the wash process) and visually appealing. If you do this yourself, you should be able to get it done for about $200 for a small lot, to maybe $500 for a larger parcel. You may find a local gardening club or someone with a green thumb to help you out, or at least provide some suggestions.

Employees

Although we go into much greater detail about employees in Chapter 8, we're mentioning the topic here because you're going to want to give some thought to the role your employees will play in the overall setup of your wash. How many will you need and for what shifts? Will you hire full- or part-time employees?

Most owners pay their workers a few dollars above the federal minimum wage. According to a recent survey by *Professional Carwashing & Detailing*, a typical starting wage was $6.46 an hour, which is just about in line with what the entrepreneurs we interviewed are paying. Generally, this rate will be higher in larger cities or places with lots of competition for the same labor pool, and lower in rural areas or in places where the supply of workers outstrips the demand. In addition, some of your employees will need to be paid at higher rates depending on the functions they perform (see Chapter 8).

Financing Your New Wash

Most new car wash owners are going to need some type of financing to get started. Earlier, we included the basics for a business plan. It is very difficult to get financing without such a detailed business plan in place. As suggested earlier, visit web sites that have business plan templates, such as www.bplans.com, buy a book specifically on writing a business plan (or take one out of the library), or buy business plan software.

In Chapter 9, there's a fairly detailed discussion of rate of return, or return on investment (ROI). This is one of the main areas where that number is going to come into play and here's why: Borrowing money to finance a new business makes sense if you can expect to earn more of a return to repay that loan. In other words, if you obtain a loan at 9 percent interest, you had better hope to make more than a 9 percent rate of return from your car wash. Otherwise, what's the point? How much more is partly a matter of opinion, but certainly you're going to want to make enough to justify the risks of investing in the somewhat risky proposition of a car wash.

As is the case with starting any new business, you can approach banks and other lenders, venture capitalists, and angel investors or borrow from friends family and personal contacts. One of the three most significant keys to success is showing the details of how your car wash will have an edge over any competitors and how you will make money, using plenty of research and realistic numbers.

The second key to success is demonstrating that this is the right business for you based on your business experience and having done your homework in the car wash field—again, the Car Wash college in Tamarac, Florida (www.carwashcollege.com), might be worth visiting for some classes. Potential investors or lending institutions like to know that the borrower has a solid working knowledge of the business that he or she is going into, therefore lowering their risk.

Finally, the third key to borrowing money is putting up some money of your own. Just as you typically need to put down money as a down payment for your home before getting a home mortgage loan, lenders are quicker to sign off on a loan if they see that you are taking some of the financial risk yourself.

Start-Up Costs for Conveyor Washes

Listed below are hypothetical start-up costs for two conveyor washes. The first is for a full-service car wash, built as a new business. The second is for an exterior-conveyor car wash bought as an existing business. These are very broad numbers and you can expect that these will vary significantly depending on the region in which you will be opening your car wash.

Start-Up Costs: Full Service	New	Existing
Cost of existing business	$ 0	$1,500,000
Building costs (including tunnel, equipment room, waiting room, and office space)	500,000	0
Land (one-month lease)	6,250 (25,000 sq. ft.)	0
Wash-related equipment (including power-wash units, vacuums, automatic dryers, water heater, water reclamation, water softener)	384,000	0
Retail/lot equipment (including shaded vacuum area, vending machines, change machines, signage, security system, trash receptacles, bathroom fixtures, cash register, lighting, inventory)	37,250	0
Office equipment and supplies (furniture, computer and software, printer, phone, fax, shredder, calculator, paper, and miscellaneous supplies)	8,050	3,000
Employee wages (for one month)	38,000	9,000
Cleaning supplies	1,900	1,200
Waxes and other protectants	700	350

Start-Up Costs for Conveyor Washes, continued

Start-Up Costs	Full-Service	Exterior-Conveyor
Other washing supplies (rags, fragrance, etc.)	$ 700	$ 350
Retail supplies (gift items, refreshments, auto accessories)	750	100
Grand opening advertising	2,000	2,000
Legal fees	1,500	1,000
Annual insurance premium	2,000	1,000
Utility hookups	7,500	7,500
Licenses and permits (including vending and business licenses)	1,000	1,000
Environmental studies and testing	2,000	2,000
Appraisal costs	1,000	1,000
Market analysis and research (demographic and feasibility studies, consultant fee, etc.)	5,000	5,000
Professional memberships	450	450
Total Start-Up Costs	**$1,002,050**	**$1,534,950**

Start-Up Costs for Self-Serve Washes

Take a look at these start-up costs for two self-serve car washes. One scenario is for building a combination self-service and in-bay automatic car wash. The other is for buying an existing self-service car wash with two wash bays.

Start-Up Costs	3 Self-Service Bays and 1 In-Bay Automatic Unit	2 Self-Service Bays Only
Cost of existing business	$ 0	$125,000
Building costs	80,000 ($20,000 a bay)	0
Land (one-month lease)	1,000 (10,000 sq. ft.)	0
Wash-related equipment (including power-wash units, vacuums, water heater, water reclamation, water softener)	99,750	0
Retail/lot equipment (including shaded vacuum area, vending machines, change machines, signage, security system, trash receptacles, lighting, inventory)	3,000	0
Office equipment and supplies (furniture, computer and software, printer, phone, fax, shredder, calculator, paper, and miscellaneous supplies)	2,615	1,000
Employee wages (for one month)	1,250 (1 part time)	0 (no employees)
Cleaning supplies	600	275
Waxes and other protectants	100	50
Other washing supplies	150	75
Retail supplies for vending machines	300	200
Grand opening advertising	500	250

Start-Up Costs for Self-Serve Washes, continued

Start-Up Costs	3 Self-Service Bays and 1 In-Bay Automatic Unit	2 Self-Service Bays Only
Legal fees	$ 500	$ 500
Annual insurance premium	1,500	800
Utility hookups	5,500	5,500
Licenses and permits (including vending and business licenses)	1,000	1,000
Environmental studies and testing	2,000	2,000
Appraisal costs	750	500
Market analysis and research (demographic and feasibility studies, consultant fee, etc.)	5,000	5,000
Professional memberships	450	450
Total Start-Up Costs	**$205,965**	**$142,600**

Inventory
and Pricing

One of the nice things about a car wash, and one of the things that attracts people to the business, is the fact that it's possible to run the business with hardly any inventory other than the supplies you need to clean cars. With that said, you may well elect to have some type of inventory beyond that—things such as air fresheners, snacks, and cleaning equipment that your customers can purchase either in a gift shop or from a vending machine.

Whatever method you devise to keep track of your inventory, the goal is always the same: To have on hand those supplies that you'll need to keep your business running smoothly and offer customers a wide selection. Therefore, you will need to establish relationships with vendors and track your inventory on a regular basis by using computer software or even in a notebook—the bottom line is always thinking ahead when it comes to what you will need, from detergent to paper goods.

In some ways there's an art to managing inventory, though most accountants would tell you they have it pretty much down to a science. As a car wash owner, nobody will know better than you what your customers want and in what quantity. Having only the bare minimum on hand or ignoring the importance of certain premium items hurts your ability to up-sell your customers.

On the other hand, there is also such a thing as overstocking. While it may seem safer to have too much than too little, it's smarter to have just enough. In this chapter, we'll get into the various methods for determining what's "just enough," and we'll look at the supplies you're going to need.

Basic Supplies for Your Car Wash

Water isn't something you inventory, neither is air if you offer vacuum services. So what will your inventory consist of? Basically, you need to think about three areas:

1. Car wash materials for the wash itself

2. Offline car-care items for sale to customers

3. Additional consumer items not related to car care.

Depending on what type of car wash you open, you may only need some of these inventory items.

- *Car wash materials:* This area begins with presoaks and detergents. You'll find various products for different purposes, such as frictionless or friction washes, different temperatures, in-bay or conveyor systems, etc. Review the presoak and detergent products very carefully in conjunction with the equipment you purchase, the type of car wash you own, and even the climate where you are located. Getting the remnants of a harsh winter off of a car may need a stronger detergent than you'll need for a good shine in Southern California. Foaming polishes and conditioners are also found in a conveyor car wash Again, there are various brands and numerous varieties to meet your needs. Sealants, drying agents, tire cleaners, and, should you offer detailing, additional products for car interiors (and other specialties) may also be part of your car wash inventory.

Additionally, any other items necessary in the process of washing a car will be part of this inventory list that must be maintained regularly.

- *Offline car-care items.* These are the things you can sell that help customers clean cars themselves, but that aren't part of your wash process. Products can be sold in a convenience store fashion or in vending machines. Air fresheners, towels, Armor All, various car cleaners, degreasers, shampoos, polishes, and waxes may be sold.

- *Additional consumer items not related to car care or "offline items."* This can consist of any type of product from snack foods and drinks to magazines, newspapers, toy cars for the kids, budget CDs, gift items, or convenience store commodities. Keep track of what sells carefully so that you aren't carrying items that just sit and gather dust.

Simple Ways to Keep Track of Inventory

To keep an eye on your inventory, you're going to need some sort of logbook or computer software that allows you to track what you've bought, what you've sold, and what you have on hand. You can probably use any one of a number of standard business software packages or get one geared specifically toward car washes.

Some of the point-of-sale software programs, such as WashSoft from Integrated Services Inc. can assist you with maintaining your inventory along with handling various other functions.

If you're buying an existing wash, you can ask the previous owner how much of each product he ordered and how often. Then you can modify his schedule over time as you notice changes in the market or the demographics. In addition, you can add products that you feel the previous owner may have missed that would work well with your customer base.

If you're starting fresh, go back to your business plan and determine how many cars you expect to wash in any given month. Then talk to your distributor or manufacturer to find out, based on that number, how much of the various supplies you're going to need. Again, if you find over time that you're consistently overestimating or underestimating what you need, make the necessary changes as you go.

Retail Items

It might be best, especially as someone who is new to the business, to start small at first if you plan to offer items not directly related to car washing. To see how you can manage your inventory of these items effectively, let's take air fresheners as an example. These are pretty popular with many car wash customers. Let's say you buy 100 air fresheners for $25 and initially price them at $1 each. In the first week you

Decisions, Decisions

When you start making inventory decisions, one of the first questions you will probably face is what to offer besides your basic wash services. Do you want to offer auto supplies (air fresheners, cleaning products, etc.), refreshments, food, or some other products you think would be helpful to your customers?

One thing you want to keep in mind when making this decision is your profit margin on each item. In some ways, this may turn out to be even more important than demand. Soft drinks may sell well, and it may seem like a great deal if a large supplier is willing to give you the vending machine for free. However, after you account for stocking the machine and paying for the electricity to run it, you may wind up making next to nothing in profit.

The best products to offer are those that cost next to nothing, but that have a high perceived value for your customers. Typical fare such as soft drinks and candy bars may not be the best choice. Talk to your customers and find out what they'd like to see you offer—they can often be your best source for market research. Items that have a longer shelf life than things that will spoil are also advisable, giving you more time to sell such items. Therefore, be careful with food items. You do not want to spend too much time stocking and restocking the shelves with non-car related items, because your focus needs to remain on your car wash and not on running a convenience store or a deli. If there is a substantial profit to be made in the non-car wash section of your facility, then you might want to bring in someone to manage this part of your business

offer them, you sell five. That means, on those five items, you made a total profit of $3.75. (Each product cost you $.25; you sold them for a buck, netting you $.75; $.75 x 5 items = $3.75.)

In the second week, you sell five more. Now you're beginning to realize that they may not move quickly enough at $1, and they're taking up display space from another item that's selling very well—a change holder for the dashboard, for example. This is when inventory becomes a concern, and also the point where inventory and pricing collide. You've got to move those air fresheners to make room for the change holders, so you drop the price of the air fresheners to $.50.

Finally, people start to buy them and you can use the free space to display more change holders. What has this taught you? In the future, you're going to want to order fewer air fresheners and more change holders. That's a very basic way to control inventory, but it's essentially what it's all about. You want to order enough of each item to sell it at the markup that you want.

By logging and tracking what you order, what you sell, and how much profit you make from each item, you'll start to see patterns. You'll start to realize that you could use some more change holders and fewer air fresheners, or vice versa as the case may be.

Stat Fact

According to Kate Carr, editor of *Professional Carwashing & Detailing* magazine, the average typical self-service car wash earns about $1,500 per wand bay per month.

Pricing Non-Car Wash (Offline) Items

Take a look at what others are charging for the items you're offering. If the convenience store across the street is selling a Coke for $.75, you probably aren't going to be able to sell it for $1.50. You may have some flexibility here—because you have a somewhat captive audience—but in general, the prices for these types of goods should just about match what others are charging.

If it turns out that, for whatever reason, you're able to make a much larger profit selling candy bars than Coke, you may want to drop the soft drinks and instead devote that space to selling more candy bars.

Pricing Your Services

The type of car wash you run will determine how you price your services in this respect. If you run a self-service wash, you're going to charge for the time the customer uses the equipment. If you operate an in-bay automatic, a full-service, or an exterior-conveyor wash, you're going to charge for each wash, no matter how long it takes.

Pricing at a Self-Service Wash

The first thing you want to determine is the start-up cost for the customer. In other words, how much money does he have to put into your machine just to turn it on? Generally, this is going to be around $1 to $1.50. A common cycle length for that first dollar is around four minutes. After the first cycle, you can charge the same amount for each additional four minutes, or raise or lower the price. For example, you could go with $1.25 for the first four minutes or $1.50 for five minutes. You could then charge a quarter per minute after that. Vacuum services are generally priced in the same way.

How much you actually charge will depend on:

- *Your facilities.* If the facilities are well maintained and you are using the latest in equipment, you can charge a little more.
- *Your location.* The going rate changes depending on the demographics of the area in which you are located.

- *Your competition.* The less competition you have, the more you can charge. Conversely, the more competition, the more you will need to maintain similar pricing.

What should also factor into your decision is the amount of profit you need to meet your projections. You don't want to set your prices at a point where you're not making any money, but you also don't want to price yourself out of the market.

A good rule of thumb is to visit other self-service washes in your area. Find out what they're charging, and then match or beat them if possible. If you truly have superior facilities and a far better location, you might be able to get away with charging a bit more than your competitors, but don't bank on it.

Another way to think about pricing is to figure out how much each wash cycle costs you to provide, and then what percentage above that you can add as your profit. For example, say it costs you $.65 a wash cycle in cleaning supplies, utilities, and other overhead costs. If you charge the customer $1 a cycle, you'll net $.35 a cycle—that's roughly a 54 percent markup.

Pricing at an In-Bay Automatic Wash

According to *Professional Car Washing and Detailing* magazine editor Kate Carr, the average in-bay price is just over $5. Of course you will need to consider the factors mentioned above, including location and your competitors to determine whether you will be able to charge $6 or need to charge $4. You also need to make sure that you are coming out ahead per wash with everything factored in.

To look at it another way, let's say you want a 50 percent markup over what it costs you to provide the car wash. If it costs you $3 a wash, you want to charge at least $4.50. You need to be aware of your bottom line to make sure that you're paying yourself enough money.

Pricing at a Conveyor Wash

According to Kate Carr, the average price for an exterior only conveyor wash is $6.43. For full service which might include vacuuming, maybe some window polishing and a tire shine, the average is $12.36. You could then have additional features for additional prices, such as a tire shine for $4 or a full mat wash and shampoo for $5 each, and so on. You could also put together package, which many car washes do, such as a gold package that is an exterior only wash for $12.50 that includes a soft cloth wash and air dry, machine wheel cleaning, undercarriage flush with rust inhibitor, foam polish, and a sealer wax. You could then have a silver package and so on. Each need to include enough to make the customer feel that he or she is getting something for the money, but not too much so that you are not making a profit.

Of course there are also the new express washes, with $7, $5, and even $3 washes for the bare minimum. These washes are cutting down their labor coasts (by having practically no labor) and operating on volume. The question remains whether or not they will be able to make money with very low prices.

Stat Fact
According to a recent study by the International Carwash Association, price is the number-one reason most home washers choose to forego visits to a professional wash facility.

Your Menu of Services

Deciding what services to offer is one part of the equation. Deciding how to offer them is the other. You have a couple of choices here. One choice is to list the basic price of a car wash, and then list each add-on separately along with its price. This isn't the best idea. It's better to package your services. The more decisions you force your customers to make, the less likely it is that they'll choose what you want them to choose. For example, which is easier for your customer to say: "I'll take a wash and presoak and tire cleaning and wax and spot-free rinse and undercarriage protection and rust inhibitor," or "I'll take the deluxe package?"

The best way to construct your menu of services is to look at other car washes—not just competitors but all over the country for some ideas. Then determine which features you believe people want the most. Have a basic package that includes a few items and then expand with larger packages from there. Keep pricing in mind. Add up the cost to you and then add up how much you can get for each feature. Be careful, because if you price your packages too high, you'll lose customers. You need to find the right balance whereby you are providing several services for a reasonable price but are also making money on the deal. You can also have some a la carte items so that you give customer some flexibility. Hint: don't overdo it. Three or four packages clearly listed and a few a la carte possibilities are all the customer will read. If it becomes overwhelming to figure out or for a greeter to explain, people won't return. Therefore, everything needs to be easily viewable on a sign and easily explained by a greeter.

You can get creative with the names you attach to your packages as well. There's no reason you have to stick with the old stand-bys like "Basic Package" or "Deluxe Wash." Instead, why not try and incorporate some type of theme into your names? For example, one car wash owner who's located in a town with a large military population named one package the "Ship Shape Super Wash." Another owner who's located in a historic mining town tried "The 49er Protectant Plus," "Gold Miner Deluxe," and "Gold Pan Basic." Yet another owner, located near a space center in Texas, named his wash packages after various lunar missions—Mercury, Gemini, Apollo, etc. His deluxe package is called "Ultimate Splashdown." This can work especially well if the names of your wash packages are somehow tied into the name of your car wash itself. Not only does it make things more interesting for customers, but it can also help the name of your wash stick in their minds. Give it some thought. We're sure you'll come up with something just as creative.

There are some other techniques you can try to draw attention to your higher-priced packages. For instance, it's a proven fact in the advertising field that the word "free" is by far the most effective at attracting the attention of customers. You might try using this as part of your signage. Let's say, for example, that after researching the competition and running through your own numbers, you decide to set the price for a deluxe wash package at $12. Let's also assume that this package includes the basic exterior wash plus rust inhibitor, special wheel cleaning, wax, hand drying, and an interior vacuum. Those are the services you're going to provide for 12 bucks no matter how you shake it. So why not call the interior vacuuming a free bonus? Or the wax, or the wheel cleaner, or whatever? Now, instead of your menu simply reading something like:

Deluxe Wash $12 includes:
Full exterior wash, wheel brightener, wax, rust inhibitor,
hand dry, and interior vacuuming.

Now it reads:

Deluxe Wash $12.00 includes:
Full exterior wash
Wheel brightener
Wax
Rust inhibitor
Hand dry
PLUS FREE INTERIOR VACUUMING

Which approach is more effective? Which is more likely to give the consumers the feeling that they've truly gotten their money's worth? You can guess. Also note that the second sign has the list going down rather than across, so the eyes can see it more easily. And it appears to have more items.

Now that you've had your fill of inventory and pricing issues, we're going to turn to another topic essential to running a successful car wash. In the next chapter, we'll tackle all the major issues that come with hiring employees for your car wash.

Car Wash
Employees

Probably the only type of car wash business that won't require you to hire employees is a self-service car wash. And even then, there will be times when you need to have someone on the premises. Even the latest in express wash facilities need some employees, although not many. In-bay automatics also should have an employee on hand at all times to make sure everything continues to work properly—remember, you are at the mercy of your equipment, and if someone breaks it, you lose more business than you'll pay someone to stay on duty.

Most evidence suggests that having an attendant on duty will increase the revenue you derive from any in-bay automatics you may have installed. The duties of a self-service/in-bay automatic wash employee are not nearly as extensive as those for an exterior-conveyor or full-service wash. You might want to think of these employees as caretakers. They are available to help customers should a problem arise, answer questions about the proper way to use equipment, make change, and generally watch over the operation to make sure everything runs smoothly.

According to a recent report by the International Carwash Association (ICA), the average self-service/in-bay automatic wash used some combination of one or two part- and full-time workers to handle these tasks. In terms of what you can expect to pay for these employees, plan to spend anywhere from $12,000 to $20,000 a year in these situations for a part timer or two to have around most of the time. Of course, you may want to handle these responsibilities yourself rather than hiring someone else, provided you have the time to do so.

For exterior-only or full-service washes, you're going to need employees. The exact positions you will need to fill will vary depending on the services you offer, but in general you can expect to need greeters (also known as service writers), cashiers, technicians, and send-off workers. Certain full-service washes may also need employees to vacuum and perform other interior work. Although you may think that a process as automated as a car wash would require very little money for employees, industry statistics reveal that the truth is very different. You can expect your labor costs to be about 20 percent of total revenues for an exterior-only wash, and close to 40 percent for a full-service wash. That's quite a chunk. To understand why the costs are so high, it's important to know what these employees do and how each contributes to your business.

Greeters (or Service Writers)

These are the revenue-generating employees, especially if they're good at selling. A service writer is the person who greets customers as they pull into your wash and takes their order. While some car washes now use touchscreen menus instead, many owners prefer having a human being as a contact person. He or she can provide a smile and personal contact while upselling the services offered. Of course, you may need to provide some sales training. This means making helpful suggestions, letting customers know of specials or items they may not be familiar with that might be beneficial to their car.

One of the keys to success in the car wash business is building your traffic count. Another key is what you do with that traffic count—i.e., how well you maximize your per-car revenue. Good service writers will help you do that.

You want your service writers to have both the freedom and the incentive to up-sell your customers in a manner that demonstrates to the customer that the service writer knows what he or she is talking about and can make honest recommendations about what type of service is best for the customer's car. Mike G., a car wash owner in Carson, California, kept the existing service writers on when he bought his car wash six years ago. He could have brought in his own people and probably paid them a bit less, but he decided it wasn't worth it. Why? Simply because they knew what they were doing. They knew the regular customers, and they were good. They're still working for him today and make decent money doing it because they're successful up-sellers. How can you encourage your service writers to up-sell? Some type of incentive program is the best means of inspiring and motivating them. We'll return to this topic later in the chapter. For now, consider the potential of a greeter who can add profits to your car wash business.

Stat Fact

Nearly 50 percent of full-service car wash owners report that greeters derive between 10 and 50 percent of their compensation from commissions, according to *Professional Carwashing & Detailing* magazine. Find a level whereby you are not giving too much away but you are providing an incentive for the greeter to sell. Of course you do not want your greeters to start aggressively trying to sell anything to anyone for the sake of commissions (this is called churning in the financial world) and driving customers away—find a good balance and make sure they provide friendly service.

Service writers need to have outstanding people skills. They need to be communicators. Appearance also counts, as does a true desire to meet customers and give them the best service you can. You should be able to easily spot those traits during the job interview. Does the applicant smile? Is he or she pleasant? Does he or she speak well? Is the applicant intelligent enough to learn the business and how the wash process works? In many instances today, greeters use the handheld touchpads to punch in the customer's order so make sure they are comfortable with the equipment. Finally, can he or she take what they know about the wash and explain it to customers? If the applicant meets all those requirements, you've probably got a well-qualified candidate on your hands. Some car wash owners report that women greeters provide a welcome smile for male customers and a woman-to-woman communication for female customers that is effective and can "appear" as less "hard-selling" then some of their male counterpoints. It works for some car washes. You'll need to determine which greeters will work best for your business.

Cashiers

You know what cashiers do, so let's not waste space running through their basic duties in much detail. Above and beyond the standard duties, however, are some basic things your cashiers can do to increase your average sale for each car. Think about the last time you went in to a fast-food restaurant and tried to order something without fries. For just about anything you order (except maybe a hot fudge sundae), cashiers will ask almost without fail "Do you want fries with that?" Your cashiers could be doing the same type of thing. Not with fries, but with gift certificates, wash booklets, air fresheners, or whatever.

It's a very simple matter to train your cashiers to up-sell. Simply make them aware of the products you have that your customers might be interested in. For instance, around the holidays, you might try a big push for gift certificates or coupon books that the customer can give away as gifts. Something as simple as "We're now offering a book of coupons good for ten washes at a discount. They make great stocking stuffers," can have a dramatic effect.

Your cashiers may also be the last people your customer sees before they leave your wash. Therefore, they're in a unique position to gather information. Teach them how to do this and what you want to know to help you make your business the best it can be. For example, training your cashiers to ask the simple question "Were you satisfied with our service?" speaks volumes to your customers. You hope that your customers will all respond with a resounding "Yes." But what if they don't? What if one of them feels their

---

Payment Pointers

What will employee wages look like for the various positions you'll need to fill? Keep this comparison in mind as a general guideline.

Service writers: $$$$
(most will derive compensation from commissions on sales)

Cashiers: $$$

Technicians: $$

Send-off employees: $

You'll fill in the dollar amounts based on the going rates in your geographic region and how easy it is or is not to find reliable employees.

car isn't as clean as they would have hoped. Therein lies the real value of having a good cashier. They can help fix the problem. If something went wrong mechanically, it may have resulted in a car being washed improperly. In this instance, a good cashier will be able to solve the problem by contacting a manager or other service technician to alert that person to the situation.

If there's some other reason the customer isn't satisfied—maybe the process took too long, another employee was rude or insulting, or he or she simply doesn't feel it was worth the money—you can set guidelines for how your cashiers should deal with these types of problems. Sometimes, the remedy will be to contact you or the manager on duty to address the complaint. Other times, it may be to offer an apology and explain that the customer experienced a unique situation, that it doesn't usually take 45 minutes for a wash but that today you were surprised by the unexpected volume. Just a few simple words of understanding can go a long way toward turning a dissatisfied customer into one who gives you at least a second chance.

Using the FlexServe system, discussed on page 101, for training employees to do more than one function means you could train someone to handle the job of customer service representative, without having to add another person to the payroll.

In terms of the qualities that your cashiers should have, they're pretty much the same as those you need to look for in a service writer. You want pleasant employees who can interact with customers and make them feel welcome. Nobody wants to hand over money to a grumpy cashier. You also need to be able to trust them implicitly. After all, they're handling your money. Make sure to ask for references from previous employers and then call them. You'd be surprised how many business owners insist on obtaining references from job candidates but never do anything with the information.

> **Bright Idea**
>
> Don't leave anything to chance with your attendants. Instead of just telling them what to do, create a checklist that they can follow each and every day. Include everything they should be doing throughout the day, from sweeping the lot to inspecting hoses and equipment. This helps ensure that nothing gets overlooked.

Technicians

We're using this term as a catch-all phrase to describe everybody else who works for you, except for your send-off employees (whom we'll discuss next). These employees will be the ones doing the little extras that help your equipment do its job better. For instance, you might have a few employees applying presoak to the wheels, or even to the entire car. You may have another whose job it is to make sure the car is going through the wash in such a way that the chance for damage is minimized—someone whose job it is to remove detachable radio antennas and remind drivers to keep all windows closed, for example.

Your technicians also need to be customer-friendly, but don't need the refined people skills of employees who regularly interact with the customers, such as cashiers and service writers. Perhaps the most important quality technicians should possess is reliability. Having employees who you know are going to show up on time and do what is expected of them is important in any business. It is perhaps even more important in a business like car washing that requires shift work. Imagine a nurse who shows up late to work every day or a waiter who is consistently late for lunch service. It's the same thing with your car wash. If your presoak guy is an hour late for work, that's an hour that each and every customer who goes through your wash doesn't get the kind of quality service you want to provide.

Send-Off Employees

These are the employees who basically take care of anything that wasn't taken care of by your service writers, technicians, or other production workers. Depending on the services you offer and what the customer has purchased, these might include employees whose responsibility it is to towel dry the car when it emerges from the tunnel, vacuum the interior, clean and polish the rims and wheels, or dust and apply protectant to the interior.

These will probably be the lowest paid of all your workers, and it's probably where you're going to see the most turnover. There's not a lot you can do about it, except for some of the ways we discuss below to keep your employee turnover below average. For this reason, you're going to need a sort of ongoing training program. One of the things you may want to consider doing in this area is to hire someone who is essentially going to serve as your department manager. He'll essentially be your sergeant for the rest of

Checking Up on Employees

There are a number of services available today that—through the use of technology—assist you in screening employees. It's worth your while to have background checks done on employees so that you do not run into trouble later. Places such as Personnel Profiles at www.PersonnelProfiles.com and InfoCublic at www.infocublic.com are among several service providers that can let you know about the background, credit history, and in some cases drug history of your future employees. More details are in the Resource section.

the send-off platoon. It will be his job to train and monitor the send-off employees. In exchange for the added responsibility, you can pay him a bit more and give him a few more perks.

Depending on how much control you want to give up, you could also allow him to make his own scheduling decisions for the send-off area, freeing you up to work on marketing strategies or other ways to grow the business. He might also be the one conducting the initial interviews when you make new hires for his area.

Flexibility

One school of thought comes from Steve Okun, car wash consultant and the creator of the FlexServe method of car wash management, a leading format used by many of the newer car operations today (along with express exterior, which is one of the three components of FlexServe).

One of the strengths of the FlexServe model is flexibility in regard to employees. "It allows you to use labor in a very prudent fashion making it cost effective and being able to serve the customer with all of the things they would need, hence being able to take the customer off of the market for competition," explains Okun. This means that by training your employees to handle multiple tasks, you can plug them in when there are holes and you are busy, or have them handling other tasks that are necessary when their primary function is not needed. This allows you to make the best use out of your labor.

"It replaces full serve because it's a more prudent use of labor, it marshals labor into one area as opposed to the disjointed labor format in the traditional full service labor format," adds Okur. All of this allows you as an owner to get a greater return on your investment by cross-training your staff to be more versatile.

Where Can You Find Employees?

Now that you know what you should expect from each of your employees, we should probably talk a little bit about how to go about finding, hiring, and retaining the kind of quality people you need to make your car wash work.

College Students

You certainly aren't going to be making many trips to the college recruiting office to set up interviews with MBA graduates (unless you're looking for someone to take over full management responsibilities for your wash). However, you may be making trips to the local college to recruit the kind of part-time employees who make your wash function on a daily basis. Of course you can always simply contact the school and post something on its job board or web site.

College students can be a great source of labor for a car wash. For one thing, they're willing to work for less money than someone with a family to support. For another, their schedules are often rather flexible. The only drawback is that these flexible schedules can make your scheduling procedure a bit more complicated than if you had a pool of employees available whenever you needed them to work. If you have many college students on your payroll, you're going to have to work around their class schedules. And what about holidays? Stock your payroll exclusively with out-of-state college kids, and you may find yourself without any available workers over the Thanksgiving and Christmas holidays—not to mention spring break and summer vacation.

Retirees

At the other end of the spectrum are retirees. In fact, for many people, the label retiree simply doesn't apply. These are people who simply can't fathom the thought of spending their golden years fishing or simply relaxing. They want to work. In some ways, retirees may be even more desirable employees than college students. As a group, retirees may be more reliable. They may also be a bit more consistent, remaining available for work regardless of the time of year. Finally, because their income is most likely going to be supplemented by retirement plans or Social Security, they may be willing to accept jobs that pay a bit less.

Just as with hiring exclusively out-of-state college students, there is a drawback to hiring only retirees. For one thing, their physical stamina may not match up to some of your younger crew members. This isn't always going to be the case, but you can generally assume that a 19-year-old is going to be able to handle more physically demanding labor than a 70-year-old. You might also run into a situation where retirees miss more work due to illnesses.

Recent Immigrants

Immigrants, both young and old, also make up a sizeable portion of the car wash work force. There may be any number of reasons for this, but certainly one of them is that a car wash job provides an entry into the work force, with relatively few specialized skill requirements.

The drawbacks? Well, one of them could be the language barrier. You would hope that anyone you hire has at least a working command of the English language, if for no other reason than to allow you to train them. You can alleviate this problem by learning a common foreign language yourself or hiring managers or other employees who are bilingual and who can help you communicate. Make sure immigrants have working papers or are citizens. Hiring illegal immigrants can come back to haunt you and cost you in fines. Consider yourself warned.

Other Sources of Labor

> **Stat Fact**
> According to a report from the International Carwash Association, full-service washes employ about three times as many employees as exterior-conveyor washes. They obviously need to charge more for such services to cover the additional wages.

If you expect to have any kind of life at all outside of your car wash, you're eventually going to have to hire someone who can function as an assistant manager to hold down the fort when you're not there. Running a car wash certainly isn't rocket science, but it isn't flipping burgers either. You may get lucky and find a student who, after working with you for a while, decides he'd like to make a career out of it. In such a case, maybe you can start training that employee on the finer points of running the business, grooming him so that one day you'll feel comfortable giving him the keys to the store, so to speak.

If not, you're going to have to find that type of employee somewhere else. Ideally, you'd be looking for someone with some managerial and business experience. It would be nice if that person was a college graduate, but it probably isn't required if he or she has some experience in the business or professional world.

The old method of taking out a want ad in the local paper certainly couldn't hurt. Using the internet job boards can also be a benefit. In some cases you may find individuals who are simply looking for steady work in what is still a somewhat unsteady economy. This may be someone who is taking courses at night to pursue a professional career or someone who is returning to work. Sometimes a woman who took time off to raise children wants to take a job once the kids are grown, and she could certainly join the team as a greeter or cashier, not that a woman on a technical job is unheard of—however, it is still far less common.

Perhaps there is a family member who wants to get into the business or you have friends who know someone responsible who would be interested. In some cases, you'll find recent graduates from high school or college who want to get some work experience under their belts. Local high schools and community colleges might be another place to look. It's highly unlikely that you're going to turn over control of your business to a 17-year-old kid, but after you spend some time training him and start to get a feel for whether or not he's trustworthy and as dedicated to the business as you are, you might find he would make an ideal assistant manager.

You can also explore job fairs or other standard recruiting opportunities, and even put help wanted signs around your wash. Many top business consultants and recruiting experts will tell you that you should never stop recruiting. Even if you think you're fully staffed, it can never hurt to hire an employee who can help you grow your business. It is also important that you have extra names, numbers, and resumes on file in case you have a sudden opening.

Rules and Regulations

Businesses are, by law, required to have employer identification numbers and to file and pay necessary taxes, workers compensation, Social Security (FICA), and so on. Here is a short list of what you need to know before hiring employees.

1. You need to obtain an EIN (employer identification number).
2. You must register with your state's labor department.
3. A payroll system must be in place for withholding taxes that need to be paid on schedule.
4. You'll need to inquire about—and (depending on the number of employees) get—workers' compensation insurance.
5. There will be required notices pertaining to safety and employee law. Make sure these are properly posted.
6. You should have software or simply a notebook in which to keep all employee data.
7. You will need to run background checks and make sure all of your employees are of working age, have proper working papers, and have Social Security numbers.
8. You should then set up an employee handbook (discussed below).
9. You may want to establish some employee benefits to remain competitive in the employment market.

Get It in Writing

You do not need a written signed contract or work agreement with an employee. However, it is in your benefit to have one that explains grounds for hiring and firing as well as the terms of employment—job title, hours, what is expected, etc. Have each employee sign such an agreement. This is protection for you in the event you have to let someone go.

10. Finally, you will need to file IRS Form 940-EZ each year and all other forms applicable to your state.

Start by contacting the department of labor in your state and the nearest IRS office to make sure you have all of the necessary paperwork. Discuss all of this with your accountant and/or attorney prior to getting started.

How to Hire the Best Employees

Now that you know where to look for employees, let's talk about how to hire the best people you can find. After reading the sections above, you should have a good idea of the traits you're looking for. Use that as the basis to write a job description. Not only will this help an applicant know if he or she is qualified for the position, it will also help you evaluate each candidate. If you're simply flying by the seat of your pants, you'll probably tend to overlook an important point here or there—add up all those mistakes and eventually you're going to have one sorry work force.

Under the Table—Not!

The public often seems to think that car washes are full of employees who are "off the books." You may assume that paying employees under the table is a convenient escape from the paperwork and regulations you have to wade through to hire someone legally. You might be tempted to take the easy way out and employ a few nonessential employees in this manner. So here's a word of advice: Don't!

The headaches you might avoid by hiring employees illegally are nothing compared to the headaches you'll suffer if you're ever caught. For example, an employee who works for you off the books can, at just about any time, turn you in. If this happens, not only will you pay fines, but you'll be required to pay all the back taxes you should have paid—plus interest for the time that employee worked for you. It's even worse if one of these employees gets hurt on the job.

As one car wash owner puts it: "When you keep an employee off the books, you have a silent partner." Why? How can you fire or reprimand one of these employees when you know how easy it can be for them to get you in serious trouble with the government? It's almost like you're asking them to blackmail you. They have you over a barrel, and that's a position no business owner wants to be in.

Identify the pros and cons of each position. It's important to be upfront with your potential employees. No one wants to come into a job expecting the possibility of a promotion only to find out six months later that none exists. Similarly, if you're open to the possibility of an employee moving up the chain in your organization, point that out. It can be a powerful selling point and one that can help sway qualified candidates to work for you as opposed to taking a dead-end job in another field.

You also want to be as honest as you can about the hours and work required. If hard, physical labor is required, tell them right away. If they're going to be standing in a tunnel hosing down cars, they're going to want to know that before they show up for their first day of work. It's also important to be clear about what they will be paid and how you plan to operate your review process—i.e., when they will be eligible for a raise and what it will take for them to get there.

Take some time to think about how you'll advertise your job openings. You're going to want some way to screen out candidates who aren't qualified right off the bat. If you can take a quick look at a resume or spend five minutes on the phone with someone, it's better than having to drop what you're doing for a half-hour interview with someone you're likely to reject. Make your job description concise and include the attributes you are looking for in an employee. Don't overdo it and make your qualifications completely unrealistic.

Once you've been in business for a while, you'll probably start to see a pattern—perhaps most of your best employees come from the local community college, for example. If that's the case, now you can possibly forego the cost of advertising and work with the college to post job openings.

You can also use your existing employees as recruiters. Many companies offer incentives to their employees to bring qualified people into the business. Perhaps you could offer a $50 bonus to any employee who brings a worker to you after that person has worked with you for a certain period of time, say three months. This can be a great strategy, as long as you have good employees in the first place.

Overcoming the Dead-End Job Stigma

Let's face it. Most kids do not grow up dreaming of working at a car wash. Whether it's deserved or not, the car wash industry certainly suffers from the perception that jobs in the industry are mostly of the low-paying, dead-end variety. In fact, ask most people on the street and they'd probably put these jobs somewhere near being an overnight janitor on the great-jobs-to-have ladder. This is a stigma that you, as a car wash owner, are going to have to overcome.

The best you can do is point out what the job can do to benefit employees and sell them on the positives, which include:

1. Work experience and, in some cases, room to advance.
2. Flexible schedules, in some cases, and part-time hours if necessary.
3. A place to hone basic work skills as well as technical skills.
4. Steady work for someone looking to earn money.
5. A growing industry with plenty of high-tech equipment. This is a plus for anyone who wants to learn about how the business works, because there is a lot of software to learn about in the car wash business.

It's very hard to convince someone starting out at a car wash (or at most service or retail jobs) that there is a great future if they stay put. Most employees at any car wash, supermarket, fast food restaurant, or even fine dining establishment, for that matter, will not be there for many years to come—unless they move to a managerial position. However, gaining practical experience and leaving the door open to a potential future in the industry (let them know about the growing industry) can provide encouragement to offset the dead-end job stigma.

How Do You Retain Employees?

We're all motivated by different forces. For some people, simply the satisfaction in knowing that they've done a job well is enough. For others, praise might be a motivator. But one thing just about everyone is motivated by is—you guessed it—money.

A Unique Tip

Instead of distributing tips at the end of each day or week, try a different and unique approach. Put them in a savings account, let them grow and earn interest, and then distribute them at the end of the year—possibly as a holiday bonus. This has a couple of advantages. For one thing, it builds the amount of money your employees earn because they'll be earning interest on the money all year long. For another, it might help slow the revolving door of employees by giving your workers an extra incentive to stick around (at least until the end of the year). To make sure the money is distributed fairly, you should come up with a simple formula that compensates workers based on the number of hours or shifts that they worked during the year. You can even post a bulletin board or poster that tracks contributions to the tip fund and shows their value every other week (or month, or whatever you choose).

We've already talked in general terms about the need to compensate your employees fairly, lest you run the risk of creating a revolving door powered by an unmotivated and surly lot of employees who your customers may dread encountering on your lot.

But base pay is really only one part of the equation. There's also the question of incentives—those little perks you offer that allow employees to boost their compensation above and beyond their standard pay. Lots of car wash owners have some type of incentive program for their employees because it allows owners to motivate employees by tying their financial success directly to the success of the business. But in order for this to work, you have to design your program so that it has maximum impact.

What Do You Want Your Incentive Program to Accomplish?

The first step seems obvious, but it's one that is sometimes ignored. In order for any incentive program to work, you have to know what it is you're trying to accomplish— what it is you're asking employees to do. For example, increasing revenue is certainly always a goal for any business, but it's not really something specific enough to ask your employees to work for. Rather than a broad, general goal that your employees will have trouble quantifying, you might try offering incentives tied to the number of super-duper-grand-deluxe washes your service writers sell.

Think about the difference that makes. If your employee knows he or she is going to get $1 for every customer who orders your most expensive wash, he or she will do more to up-sell your services. If, instead, your greeter is working toward some vague notion of increasing revenues for the company (without any real concrete idea of a personal benefit) that same motivation might not be there. You could also offer a flat bonus to an employee who exceeds a certain level of sales or sells a certain number of high-priced packages. Another option might be to offer a percentage of the sales or a percentage of sales once receipts reach a certain level. These options are a bit more complicated than the simple "one wash, one buck" system, but they still let employees know that their success is tied to how well the business does.

There are other areas that you might want to target for incentive programs. Customer service is an important one. These can be a bit harder to administer because the concept of good customer service is somewhat subjective. You can try things like comment cards, but these might turn out to be a bit unwieldy to deal with. You can also try to simply evaluate the general level of service you see over a certain period of time, and distribute "bonuses" to all your line workers based on how you feel they've performed over the past week or month. Another option would be to use your creativity in developing a program everyone can understand. For example, maybe you could put $10 into a fund for every day that is free of customer complaints, and then distribute the money at the end of every month to all your employees, based on how much they worked that month.

If you offer incentives, remember that they have to be large enough to mean something to your employees. The bottom line is that you're asking your employees to work harder so that your business does better financially. Show them you appreciate the effort and share the wealth. Think of it this way: If your employees can increase sales by 2 percent, even if you gave them back 15 percent of that increase in revenues, you'll still be ahead.

Health Insurance and Benefits

Ask most car wash owners and they'll tell you that, more and more, they're finding it essential to offer benefits to their employees to attract the kind of competent, reliable employees they need. Medical and dental insurance are often at the top of the list of desired benefits and, in fact, a reason people will chose one job over another, because the long talked about plan for national health benefits may never come to fruition. It's no secret that medical and medical insurance are becoming incredibly expensive, so it will definitely pay to shop around to see if you can scare up any deals.

One avenue you might want to look into is getting insurance through a local organization that you belong to. A logical choice would be your chamber of commerce. You can also try national organizations such as the National Federation of Independent Business. Once you're a member, you may be eligible to buy insurance at a reduced rate. Also look for car wash associations in your region. The International Car Wash Association may be a place to start (www.carcare.com or 888-ICA-8422).

Training Programs

Your employees, unless they have some previous car wash experience, are probably going to come to you completely green. Everything they know about the car wash business is going to come from you. This means you're going to need a training program. Keep these guidelines in mind as you design one:

- Don't simply teach how; also explain why you are doing something.
- Define objectives clearly.
- Lead by example.
- Ask for questions often.
- Do not make assumptions that everyone is at the same place on the learning curve (in fact, make sure everyone understands the language—if not, you will need to find someone who is bi-lingual to help you).

Technical Training

To begin with, your employees need to be taught how everything works. You don't need to teach them enough so that they will know how to fix the machinery in a pinch (though that would be nice, wouldn't it?). But they should have a working knowledge of the basic process involved in washing a car and how to spot small problems before they become big ones.

For a full-service or exterior-conveyor wash, any training program you initiate should include a walk through your tunnel (when it's not operating, of course) during which you can point out the various pieces of equipment, what they do when they're working properly, and what they might do if they malfunction. For a self-service or in-bay automatic wash, you're going to want to take them into your equipment room and around the bays and machinery to demonstrate the process.

Customer Service Training

This may be even more important than the technical stuff. Unfortunately, dealing with people in a respectful and helpful way doesn't come naturally to some people. We're talking about employees who may be very dedicated to their work, but who, for one reason or another, are not the best when it comes to interacting with customers. If

---

Can We Talk?

There's nothing like a busy conveyor wash. The first time you see a long line of cars stretching from the entrance to your tunnel, you're going to know why you got into this business in the first place. But with your good fortune come a few problems that you're going to have to solve. One of these is communication. What's the best way to relay information from your service writers, who may be busily working taking orders far away from the tunnel, to the technicians who are actually operating the equipment? It sounds like a minor detail, but it's a vitally important question. If your employees are messing up orders, it can create confusion and a slowdown, resulting in lost customers and profits.

For this reason, give some thought to the best way for your employees to talk to each other and relay information about customers on your busiest days. Some washes use a simple bar of soap to write orders on a customer's windshield. You can also try washable or dry-erase markers to accomplish the same thing. Another way to do it, if you're a bit leery about writing on your customer's cars, is to give each of your service writers a kind of ticket book. They can write orders on the tickets and place them under the windshield for your other employees to see. Of course, as noted earlier, there is increasing usage of the high-tech touch-pad systems that print out the items for the customer and even relay them to another part of your facility.

---

you have enough of these employees, you may have the smoothest-running car wash in town with the least volume of cars actually passing through it.

Beware!
Be careful about who you hire as an employee. One owner told us a story about an employee who broke equipment on purpose so that he would get overtime to fix it. Look for unusual activity and patterns.

In an increasingly impersonal world, one with numerous recorded phone messages that lead to nine or ten prompts and increasing hi-tech interactions, customer service is becoming more and more significant. For that reason, customer service training is an important step in your business development. Training your people to be great with customers doesn't just mean requiring that they greet every customer with a "Good morning, welcome to Al's car wash"—although that's certainly a start. It also means teaching them how to listen to customers carefully and to follow through when a complaint is made. One of the difficulties here is that this directive will sometimes contradict your other major goal—to wash as many cars as possible.

Let's face it, there will be smooth days and days where problems have to be resolved. These problems will eat up some of your time and resources that could otherwise be spent making money. But you can't think of it that way and neither can your employees. Remember, in nearly every business, it is much, much cheaper to hold on to existing customers than it is to go out and replace customers who won't become regulars because of a bad experience they had at your wash. Instead, your employees must be trained to take each customer complaint or concern seriously.

Your employees should be trained to recognize that a complaint is not a bad thing in all circumstances—instead, it's an opportunity to create a truly satisfied customer. Don't get us wrong, we're not saying you should intentionally solicit complaints from customers. But what we are encouraging you to do is to not necessarily view them as a negative. On the contrary, there can often be nothing more satisfying than doing your best to please an unhappy customer and turning him around from a liability to an asset.

So train your employees to welcome all comments—positive and negative. Give them an idea of common customer service complaints they'll encounter and how to resolve them. Give them the power to make things right when a customer isn't happy. Heck, give them a $5 bonus every time they solve a customer problem or bring it to you, if they can't solve it. Let employees know that while there are rules, guidelines, and regulations, there are also ways to solve problems that may be unique and may not fall within the usual guidelines. The phrases, "That's what the computer says" or "we have to do it that way, it's our policy" or the classic, "If we do that for you, we'll have to do it for everyone" are not very customer service friendly and can lose business. Do whatever it takes to ensure that you do whatever you can to have every customer leave your wash happy, satisfied, and ready to spread the word about your great business.

▲

Turning Over Responsibilities

There's probably going to come a time when you decide to turn over the day-to-day managerial responsibilities of your wash to one of your employees. That's not a guarantee—you might love the work so much that you can't imagine someone else doing it—but if you decide to open another wash, take a vacation, or simply retire from the daily grind, someone is going to have to step in and do all of the mundane things you've been handling.

How do you decide which of your employees will get the keys to the shop? Here are some of the characteristics you should look for in anyone you are considering selecting as a managerial employee to fill in for you:

- *Financial responsibility.* Most of your business is transacted in cash. It's very easy for some of it to go missing if it's not in the right hands.

- *Respect of the other employees.* Employees must treat the manager with the same respect they show you.

- *Respect of the customers.* If customers have gotten to know the employee and like him, they won't hesitate to remain loyal to your business.

- *Honesty.* You need to know that if your manager tells you something happened, it's as good as if you saw it happen with your own eyes.

- *Ambition.* A good manager wants to prove to you, and to himself, that he can do a good job running the business.

- *Attention to detail.* You built your business by making sure everything ran like a well-oiled machine. Someone needs to pay as close attention to the little things as you did.

- *Dependability.* This is a trait that the employee you're considering should have displayed over the entire time he spent working for you.

There may be other factors that play into your decision, too. It could be that you don't think any of your existing employees fit the bill, and you have to go outside to find a manager. You can try luring away an experienced car wash manager from another business by promising a bit more money. That may work, but remember this: If he joined you for more money, he could also leave you for more money. Then you'd be right back at square one. It also shows other employees that you do not promote from within, which is a major morale buster and a way to lose a good "up-and-comer."

Smart Tip

Tip...

Always maintain a list of on-call workers to replace any regularly scheduled workers who don't show up for their shift. If you use the FlexServe method, you should be able to move a person from one job to cover another. Maintain a list of the various skills each person can do once he or she is cross-trained.

Whatever you decide, it's important that you're extremely comfortable with the decision you make. Nothing is worse than lying in bed at night wondering how well your business is being run.

Knowing When to Let Them Go

There probably isn't a business in the United States that hasn't had to fire an employee at some time, and your car wash probably isn't going to be any different. Firing someone is never a pleasant task, but if you're going to run a business, you're going to have learn how to do it correctly to safeguard yourself.

Lest we remind you that we are living in a very litigious society. If a woman could sue a fast-food restaurant for millions of dollars because she spilled a cup of coffee on herself—and settle out of court for big bucks—then you'd better believe that you can be sued for wrongful termination. It happens all the time.

Knowing how to conduct a job interview, presenting a hiring contract (to be signed by the employee), and having a comprehensive employee manual will give you some protection. It will provide you with a form of backup in writing, indicating that the employee had knowledge of what conduct was expected of him or her. If you follow the guidelines set forth in the manual and adhere to your requirements for what constitutes an "on-the-spot" firing, you will be in a much better position should you need to defend your actions. It's pretty hard for employees to complain that they were fired incorrectly if you can document a clear violation of the rules as set out in writing in the employee manual. You should have each employee sign that he or she has received the manual, so that the employee cannot say "I never got one."

What actually determines when it's time to fire an employee is pretty much up to your discretion, but the point is that it should be done following a set of guidelines that you've set down and of which your employees are well aware. Take a look at the section "Developing Your Employee Manual" (below) for elements to include in your employee manual.

How should you conduct what's come to be known as "the exit interview"? In a word: carefully. Remember, you're not trying to create an enemy here. You certainly don't want someone with an inside knowledge of your business to hold a serious grudge against you. You can offer to help them find a job somewhere else where their skills might be more appropriate or make clear that you won't give a negative recommendation to any potential employer who calls. Of course, you don't want to lie on the former employee's behalf, but you can let it be known that you can part on amiable terms and that such a parting can benefit the employee when he or she needs a future job reference. While you are not required to tell an employee why he or she was let go, you can provide a general explanation. Hint: Prepare it ahead or time and have your lawyer review it (unless your lawyer is the one you are firing).

Developing Your Employee Manual

Despite what popular misconceptions lead us to believe, hiring a car wash employee entails a lot more than just tossing a few dry rags at someone and telling them to get to work. Employees need to be taught what is expected of them and be informed of behaviors that will not be tolerated. This is important, not just because it helps your business run more smoothly but because it can also save you the headache of a lawsuit if an employee feels he or she was fired for no good reason. One way to accomplish this is with a well-thought-out employee manual. You'll probably want to consult an attorney about exactly what kinds of things should go into your employee manual, but here are some ideas to get you started.

- *Wash processes.* Describe in detail exactly what happens when a car disappears into the tunnel, if you're running a full-service or exterior-conveyor wash, or the process for washing a car yourself if you're running a self-service wash. When employees know what's going on, they're better prepared to assist customers if they have any questions or if something goes wrong.

- *The equipment.* Explain what the equipment does and how it works. You don't need to go into the kind of detail a mechanic would need, but a general overview of how the equipment functions can help an employee spot potential problems and also answer basic customer questions.

- *Your menu of services.* This may change a bit from time to time as you expand into other areas or drop services that aren't contributing to your profits, but you should be able to give a general overview of the services you provide. Break each level of service down, and explain each of the components.

- *Your mission statement or philosophy.* There's almost no doubt that you'll have this information posted in other places besides your employee manual, but there's no reason why it shouldn't be part of this document as well.

- *Customer payment.* Let employees know what forms of payment are acceptable and how to handle checks (asking for types of IDs). Employees should also know the procedure for redeeming gift certificates or special coupons and what to do in case a credit card is rejected.

- *Customer complaints.* Spell out exactly what is expected of an employee who receives a customer complaint. Who should be notified? How should it be handled? By explaining the process now, you reduce the chance of a conflict down the road.

- *Tipping or commission policy.* For most of your employees, tips or

Stat Fact
The average full-service wash employs just over 30 people in a given year.

other forms of non-salaried payment are probably going to be part of their compensation. Take the opportunity to spell out the program in your employee manual (though you may want to have another document that goes into even greater detail).

- *Uniforms and appearance.* Assuming that your employees will be required to be in uniform (and they should be), you will need to spell out exactly what it means when you say they must show up to work "in uniform." You should also state at least some basic policy about jewelry and personal appearance/hygiene.

- *Employee absenteeism.* You should make it clear that employees are expected to show up for work on time when they're scheduled. They must notify you if they are sick or cannot come in, prior to the start of the work day or of the shift. If you allow for a certain number of "sick days" with pay, spell that out. Explain that x number of additional days absent can be grounds for termination.

Beware!
When you find it necessary to discipline employees, make sure you document everything that is said and save it. This can help prevent complaints and lawsuits later on if you find it necessary to terminate their employment. Also, make it a habit not to discipline employees in front of one another, it leads to low morale. Call an employee aside or ask him or her to speak with you in your office.

- *Employee scheduling.* Explain how the scheduling system works, as well as where and when the schedule is posted each week. This section might also include your policy on schedule requests and vacations—i.e., how requests are made, how the manager or owner determines whether to deny or accept the request, etc. Make sure that all of your scheduling policies are very clear in regard to employees switching shifts, and so on.

- *Harassment policy.* This is one you're almost definitely going to need a lawyer to help you with, but the point is that no employee will at any time harass another employee, customer, or vendor. This includes sexual harassment. There's no room for ambiguity here. Make clear what steps employees should take if they feel they are being harassed (i.e., who should be notified about the incident, what steps will be taken, etc.). You should also indicate how the company will act to determine the merit of the accusation and what steps will be taken against the offending party if the complaint is found to have merit, which will likely be immediate termination.

- *Reprimand schedule.* One of the ways to protect yourself against claims that an employee was terminated unfairly is to spell out in specific detail how you plan to reprimand employees who break the rules. A typical reprimand schedule might be a verbal warning for the first violation, followed by a written warning and perhaps the loss of a shift (or some other "pocketbook penalty") for a second violation. A third violation would most likely result in termination. Again, this is an area where you should consult an attorney, but those are some general guidelines many businesses follow.

- *Termination policy.* This section should cover not only what constitutes grounds for termination but also what you expect if the employee decides to quit. Although there's really no way to enforce it, you should require that employees give at least ten days' notice that they'll be leaving. This will give you enough time to shift your schedule to ensure that you don't wind up short on busy days. You can probably increase the likelihood that an employee will honor the notice period by making it clear that any positive recommendations to future employers are dependent on the employee leaving your business on good terms. You also need to make it clear that all keys and materials belonging to the business must be returned upon termination or if an employee should quit.

- *Drug policy.* Aside from the legalese you'll most likely have to insert in this section, the main point you want to get across is that showing up for work while under the influence of alcohol or drugs and being in possession of any illegal substance while in your employ is grounds for immediate termination. This is important not only because of the image your employees project to your customers but for safety reasons as well. Obviously, an employee under the influence is much more likely to hurt himself or others than one who shows up clean and sober. Discuss drug testing policies with your attorney before asking someone to take a drug test. There are various employee rights that you must be aware of.

- *Theft policy.* This needs to be worded carefully, but the idea that stealing from the business will result in immediate termination should be spelled out.

- *Discount policy.* As an added perk, you may want to grant free or reduced wash privileges for your employees. You can also extend that privilege to immediate family members if you're feeling generous. If you decide to offer this, you're probably going to want to set limits. Perhaps you can limit the discount to a particular day of the week which experience has shown to consistently be your slowest day. You'll also want to limit the number of times the discount can be used—twice a month for example.

- *Evaluation and raises.* Let employees know exactly how they will be evaluated, when (after 3, 6, or 12 months), and when they can anticipate a possible raise.

- *Benefits.* Clearly spell out when the employee becomes eligible for any benefit package, how the package works, and what happens if he or she leaves the company.

- *Equal opportunity statement.* A simple statement to the effect that your business does not discriminate on the basis of sex, religion, race, disability, or sexual preference will probably suffice for this section, although your attorney should be the final word here.
- *Other points to cover.* Other sections of your manual might include an employee smoking policy (where and when it's allowed, if at all), what sections of your wash are off limits except to managers (equipment rooms or the office, for example), where and when employees may use their cell phones, and the procedure for making recommendations or lodging complaints with a manager.

Interviews

Prior to interviewing job applicants, it is important that you have your employee handbook printed and reviewed by your attorney. It is also important that if you are planning to have a hiring agreement, that it is ready in advance of offering an employee a position.

You also need to be prepared prior to the interview and know which questions you will ask and what you want to learn about each applicant. The idea is to get an overall feel for his or her past experience, attitude, aptitude, and overall personality. You may want to find out what he or she hopes to do in the future (goals or aspirations). Questions that ask how the person will react in various situations can give you an idea of whether or not they can handle making quick decisions or dealing with problems that may arise.

A resume may show that someone has been a cashier for five years, but it may not show whether or not the individual has the people skills you would like from your cashier. You need to evaluate both skills and the personality/character of the individual.

During the interview, you should explain the basics of the car wash business, the nature of the job, the responsibilities, and what is expected of the employee. You should ask a few specific questions and jot down notes as the applicant responds. You should have their resume in front of you. It is a good idea to have each applicant fill out a basic application form with the essential information (name, address, phone number, previous employment, schooling, and so on) to save time. Keep it fairly simple.

Remember to not only check references but also to take some time to do a background check before hiring employees. References are good, but applicants for a job will inevitably put down the names of other people whom they know will say good things about them.

Always ask an employee if it is okay if you contact his or her previous (or current) employer. In fact, get that in writing on the application form.

▲

Also remember that you cannot ask questions about the personal life of the applicant. That means you need to avoid questions such as whether or not the applicants are married, their religions, sexual preferences, ages, etc. Likewise you cannot make any references, insinuations, or comments about the personal life of the individual. Be careful with both questions and comments. You can ask if someone is over the age of 18, for legal reasons.

Income and
Expenses

Finally! Now we're going to talk specifically about how much money you can make in this business. There is a very specific process for determining your anticipated revenue. It involves lots of number-crunching and research, but it's an absolutely vital part of the process for finding out whether or not your new business will be able to survive.

▲

To some extent, the decision on whether or not to proceed with your specific car wash business is a subjective one. The so-called fringe benefits of owning your own business may be paramount in your mind, and as long as you can make a living doing it, that may be enough. But usually you're going to want to get a bit more out of it. In addition, assuming that you're going to need a loan to get started, the bank will want to see that you're going to be able to survive financially before it grants your loan.

Evaluating Risk

Investing in anything involves some amount of risk. Contrary to what many people believe, the definition of risk is a lot broader than you may think. For example, it's easy to see what the risk is when you invest in the stock of an unproven, highly speculative new company. Following that train of thought, you'd probably say that it's a bit less risky to invest in a blue-chip stock, safer still to invest in government bonds, and virtually foolproof to invest in a bank certificate of deposit, or simply to keep your money in a savings account. That's the way most people look at risk. But in economic terms that's not entirely accurate, and here's why. When you tie your money up in a low-yield investment such as a CD, you're risking your ability to earn higher returns through another form of investment. What all this means is that even what you may consider to be the safest investment, may turn out to cost you money in the long run. The risk of not keeping up with the rate of inflation is also realistic. No, you may not be losing money, but, if over five years, you earn 2 percent more and inflation goes up by 3 percent, you are actually losing money. This is just another type of risk, among several.

For now though, let's stick with the generally accepted definition of risk. The less sure you are about how an investment will perform, the riskier it is. Opening your own car wash business lies somewhere near the risky end of the spectrum.

One of the reasons interest rates on bank savings accounts are so low is because there is so little risk involved. Banks can get away with paying 4, 3, or even 2 percent interest because there's virtually no chance you'll lose money. It's a whole different ballgame when you're starting a new business. You're going to be looking for a much higher return on your investment to justify the risk involved.

Your Rate of Return

Exactly what your desired rate of return should be, depends on many factors, some of which can't really be quantified (such as being your own boss). But beyond those, there are some hard and fast numbers that you'll have to consider before you jump in. For this analysis, you'll need to know how much money you can hope to make, what you're going to have to pay to make that income, and the size of your initial investment. Except for your initial investment, you're going to have to make an educated guess about the other numbers. You can use the upcoming charts as sample estimates.

Projecting Annual Revenue from an Existing Wash

If you've done your homework, you should have a pretty decent idea of how much money you can expect to take in every year. You may want to be a bit conservative in coming up with this number. Being too optimistic can lead you into making an investment in an existing wash that will be very hard to keep afloat.

If you're buying an existing wash, the current owner is probably going to be your best source of information for the kind of revenue you can expect. Be careful about assuming that once you take over and make improvements you're going to be able to dramatically increase revenue over the previous owner. Experience says otherwise. Sure, if you upgrade and modernize your equipment or clean up the exterior of the facility, you may see a slight bump in revenue—but nothing dramatic.

If you have reason to suspect that the numbers you're seeing from the current owner have been "fudged," there are ways to check their validity using other information. One way is to check water usage records for the business. Once you know how much water the site is using, you can call the equipment manufacturer to get a rough estimate of the volume of business the site should be doing. It's not an exact measure of course, but it can give you an indication as to whether or not you're getting accurate figures from the current owner.

Beware!

Don't take the previous owner's word for it. He or she is selling a business, so of course, you're are going to hear all about the positives of the business and the potential to make big money. Review the financials very carefully. Look at financial statements from the accountant or accounting firm that worked with the car wash and make sure that you are buying a business that has made money before. Also find out why the owner is selling. Look for any undisclosed reasons that may have prompted a sale, such as a new competitor opening nearby, a change in the zoning laws, a major increase in area utility rates, a change in the traffic flow, or anything else that may impact the future of the business.

Projecting Annual Revenue from a New Wash

This is a bit trickier. To get an accurate picture of what you can expect to make from a new wash that you're planning to build from scratch, you're going to need information from a wide variety of sources. First and foremost is data from places such as the International Carwash Association (ICA), *Professional Carwashing & Detailing* magazine, or local car wash associations in your neighborhood. These can provide you with information such as average annual revenues and costs for a variety of different types of washes across the country. There are also ways you can check into this kind of information on your own. This may mean driving around to various car washes in your area and simply checking out the pricing. For a full-service, exterior-conveyor or in-bay automatic wash, all you need to do is check out the car wash's menu of services. For a self-service wash, you may need to do a bit more investigating. You aren't simply looking at price; you're also looking at time. How much time in the bay does each token or each quarter buy the customer? By taking the price and dividing it by the time of the cycle, you come up with a figure that represents how much a customer is paying for a minute of washing time. That's the figure you'll want to use for projecting revenues.

Pick a pricing schedule that lies somewhere in the middle of the prices you've seen other washes charge. This will help ensure that you aren't being overly optimistic about your chances.

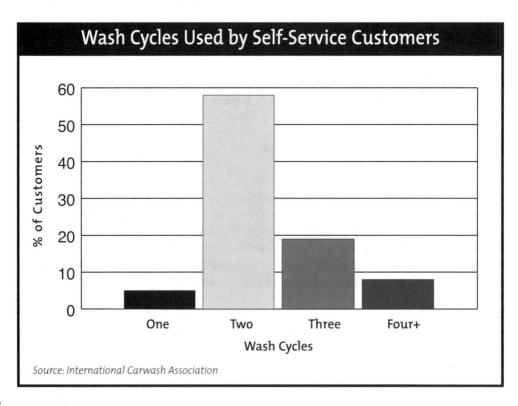

Wash Cycles Used by Self-Service Customers

Source: International Carwash Association

The next step is to determine the volume you can expect. Again, organizations such as the ICA can provide data that can help with this calculation. You can also make use of figures you obtain independently.

When checking online, or in national associations or trade magazines, make sure to look at numbers of the same type of car wash you are planning to open. Also focus on similar geographic areas. Someone opening a wash in Los Angeles is not going to get an accurate picture of pricing or volume of cars by looking at statistics from a car wash in a small town in Kansas.

For a self-service wash, what you'll want to know is how many minutes a day (on average) you can expect each bay to be in operation. This will vary from region to region, as well as from location to location. Based on surveys in publications such as *Professional Carwashing & Detailing* magazine and *Auto Laundry News*, the average minutes a day can range from less than 100 to more than 150. You can try to obtain some numbers from car wash owners in your region, as long as they are far enough away from your new site to not see you as a competitor. If you survey enough of these, you'll probably be able to come up with a fairly good estimate.

Let's take a number in the middle and say that, based on your research and independent numbers you've studied from surveys, you're assuming you can reasonably expect each of your bays to be in operation for 125 minutes a day. Multiply that by the price per minute you can expect to receive—perhaps $.40—and you come up with a figure that will tell you how much revenue you can expect each of your bays to generate on a daily basis. In this example it would be $50 a day or roughly $1,500 per month (which is just above the average for self-serve bays). Multiply that by 365 to find your annual revenue for each bay. Using the numbers we have here, that would work out to $18,250 in annual revenue per bay. Finally, multiply that by the number of bays you plan to build, and you'll have the total annual washing revenue for each bay. If you plan to open a six-bay wash, your total annual revenue would be $109,500.

Now it's time to move on to your vacuuming. The average vacuum brings in roughly $175 per month at a self service bay or $2,100 per year. Add this figure to the revenue generated from the car washing operations and you come up with $111,600.

The process for determining projected revenue for other types of washes is similar. You can also factor in the average projected revenue for a vending machine or from other items. However, keep your primary focus on the wash—if the car wash makes money, then you can add additional profit centers. However, you don't want to find yourself relying on other income sources to keep a conveyor car wash afloat because there is so much involved in running such a business. If you depend on other areas to keep the business profitable, you might as well sell the car wash and simply run a convenience or auto parts store.

You're always going to need to know how much volume you can expect, but for in-bay or conveyor car washes, instead of estimating the number of minutes a day your wash will be in operation, you're going to want to know how many cars you can expect

Smart Tip

Tip...

If you're constructing a brand-new self-service wash, try to construct your bays so that the openings have southern exposure. This will keep them warmer during cold periods, thus helping to prevent ice buildup, while simultaneously keeping down your heating costs.

to wash in any given year. This again will vary depending on your region, but surveys can give some indication of averages.

For an in-bay automatic wash—the kind you might typically find as a supplement to a self-service wash—a recent survey in *Auto Laundry News* put the average number of cars washed annually in each automatic bay at 21,337. For the purposes of streamlining an example, let's round that off to 20,000 per year. Again, this is a general average compiled from owners all across the country. Let's also assume that your wash has three automatic bays so that the total number of cars you can expect to wash in any given year is around 60,000.

Next, rather than the price per minute you expect to charge, you'll need to know the revenue you can expect to generate from each car. The average gross revenue for each in-bay customer, according to *Auto Laundry News*, is $4.48. Again rounding off for our example, let's make it $4.50. This means that your wash will generate $90,000 in revenue per bay every year. If you have three bays, the total revenue comes to $270,000.

For exterior-conveyor and full-service washes, the process for arriving at projected revenue is pretty much the same, but the numbers change. Again, location will factor into the equation along with the type of car wash you are touting. For example, a new car wash in the Los Angeles area, one of the new trend of exterior-only washes, called El Segundo Car Wash, washed 7,300 cars in its first month of business. The choices are $5 for a five-minute express wash and $11 for a top of the line wash. The following month it climbed to 12,048 customers. At this rate (an average of 9,674 per month), it would handle 116,088 cars per year!

Meanwhile, Sparkle Car Wash in Columbus, Indiana, was reopened in late 2005 and follows the FlexServe model of washing cars, providing options and using two tunnels—one for exterior-only washes and a second (as an option) offering interior cleaning. The facility is now seeing 6,000 cars per month or 72,000 per year.

Obviously, the length, speed, and location of the wash will indicate how much business you see—with these being above-average results, largely because of the exterior-only features, which increase volume but cost less per customer.

Most conveyor car washes will see between 35,000 and 65,000 cars annually. If you see 55,000 cars for exterior-only washes at an average of $5 per wash, then you will see income of $275,000. If, however, you see 40,000 cars for a full-service wash at an average of $12 each, you would see $480,000. It all depends on what you are selling and how much business you believe you can attract. While the $480,000 obviously looks more appealing, it also comes with additional labor and material costs that are not associated with the exterior-only car washes—while the FlexServe is a hybrid of sorts, offering some of each, full service and express.

While these numbers look encouraging, you will need to put them up against your expenses to get an idea of how much profit you will see.

Remember that in all these examples, we're figuring out average revenue a day. This doesn't mean that you can expect to make this every day. It simply means that at the end of the year, when you add up all the totals, this is the average of what you made on any given day during the year. There will be slow days (and slow weeks and months), just as there will be days when you get "slammed." This is an important distinction, especially if you're making loan payments that come due every month. Try telling the bank that you can't make a payment on your loan because it's your "slow time of the year." Good luck.

A Token Thought

The choice of whether or not to use tokens or money to operate your machinery is a pretty big one, and unfortunately there's no great consensus about which is better. You'll find owners who swear by tokens, just as you'll find owners who swear by sticking with cash. Here are some of the pros and cons of each approach.

If you stick with coins, anecdotal evidence suggests that you'll have more incidents of vandalism because crooks have a lot more to gain by stealing real money rather than phony money that can only be used at your wash.

However, some owners say that the drop in vandalism simply isn't worth losing customers. While there are no hard and fast statistics to back it up, these owners say that they've heard about washes that switched from coins to tokens and lost a significant amount of business—business that never came back, even when they went back to using coins.

On the other side of the coin (pun intended), tokens, in addition to cutting down on the kind of vandalism that can really cripple your wash, can make it easy to market your business. Here's why: Say, for example, that you want to try a marketing tactic like pursuing premium deals or working with a charity. It's very easy to simply sell your tokens at a discount to a third party, which can in turn resell to the eventual end-user. If you're operating under a cash system, you don't have the opportunity for this kind of arrangement—you can't sell a quarter at a discount. So if concerns over safety and the "portability" of your marketing efforts are high on your list, tokens may be the way to go. Also, if someone has extra tokens at home that work only in your wash, then they will have to return to you, rather than go to your competitor's wash.

Operating Costs

Now that we have a handle on projected revenues, we need to study operating costs. Then finally, we'll have an idea of the kind of profit-making potential your car wash will have.

How much do you estimate it will cost to run your business? Unlike the conservative approach you should take when projecting revenues, it's probably a better idea to err on the high side when estimating costs. Take everything into account here—employees, general supplies, maintenance, legal fees, insurance, etc.

For an existing car wash, an estimate is fairly simple. Take a look at the books, and this will tell you (give or take a couple of percent) what your costs are going to be. Of course, if you plan on making radical changes, such as upgrading equipment, hiring or firing a significant number of employees, or radically changing the menu of services, you're going to have to factor that into the equation.

Calculating Your Return on Investment

For this exercise you're going to need to know the size of your initial investment (i.e., how much it's going to cost to start or buy your car wash business), the projected operating costs for the business, and the projected revenue for the business.

Knowing these three things, you can now calculate what your expected annual rate of return, or return on investment (ROI), will be. You can determine this figure as follows:

- *Step 1.* Subtract projected costs from projected revenue. This gives you your estimated annual profit.
- *Step 2.* Divide your estimated annual profit by the amount of money you're going to invest. This is your ROI.
- *Example.* Consider a hypothetical four-bay, self-serve wash where you invest $100,000.

   Projected revenue = four bays x $15,000 a year = $60,000

   Projected costs = supplies and maintenance (4 bays x $5,000 a year) = $20,000

   Miscellaneous expenses (legal fees, insurance, etc.) = $12,000

   Projected profit = $60,000 – $32,000 = $28,000

   Return on investment = $28,000 ÷ $100,000 = 0.28 (or 28 percent) ROI (pretty darn good)

It's important to point out that there's no right or wrong answer here. A 10 percent ROI might be all right for some, but too low for others. What determines your own personally acceptable ROI will depend on factors such as the other investment options available to you and the non-monetary benefits you'll derive from being in business for yourself. Of course, if your ROI is zero or close to it, then it's a bad idea no matter how much of a thrill you'll get from being your own boss.

Revenue Streams

We hope this will come as no surprise: The vast majority of your revenue will come from washing cars. However, most car wash owners today supplement that income by providing other goods or services. These additional revenue streams can be vitally important. For example, some statistics put revenue from vending machines at around 15 percent of the total revenue for a self-service wash, while some put it even higher. That's pretty dramatic. For an idea of just how much this can affect your business, just think what would happen if you watched your revenue drop 15 percent in a year.

Extra services can take the form of anything from vending machines to vacuum or shampooing facilities. While it's important to recognize that the wash is your main service, don't get so focused on that aspect of the business that you lose sight of the many other profit centers available to you.

Thus far, the success of the express exterior business—which is popular and relatively new—has yet to be determined. Because many owners have just opened these facilities, the jury is still out on how profitable they will or will not become.

Gift Shops

Depending on the space you have available, you may be able to combine your wash with a small gift shop. For example, Dick H. in Sacramento, California, doesn't just sell air fresheners and fuzzy dice for your rearview mirror in his shop. He sells greeting cards (even claiming to have one of the largest selections in the area) and handbags. It may sound strange, but when you think about it, why should it be? Remember, as we've been discussing, one of the things car wash customers want is to combine getting a wash with other errands. If they can stop for a wash and then run in to pick up a birthday card, why not do it? In the end, you're really only limited by your imagination and your space in terms of what you can sell.

Adding Other Non-Car Wash Related (Offline) Services

The range of services you can offer in addition to car washes sometimes seems to have no end. For example, in addition to vending machines with your typical snack foods of chips and soft drinks, some washes have gone to even greater lengths—like setting up a real, bona-fide fast-food restaurant on the premises. While that's an expensive proposition, you could probably think of something similar to do with your wash.

Of course, you could always be more traditional and stick to selling hot dogs during lunchtime. Maybe, if you're located in an area that already has street vendors, you could invite one of them to set up shop on your lot and ask for a share of his profits. It helps the vendor because he's taking advantage of your traffic flow and a steady stream of customers. It helps you because you're making a little extra money with no additional effort. And it helps your customers because you're providing them with a service they wouldn't normally expect to find at a car wash. Of course, keep in mind that food items can sometimes be more effort than they are worth. You may look for a reliable coin-operated vending business in the area and have them supply machines. Ask for a commission from the machines and make sure they are replenished regularly.

But it doesn't stop there. Think about what other opportunities your facilities allow you to explore. For example, did you know there's a company that manufactures equipment that will allow your customers to wash their pets in one of your self-service bays? It's true. According to *Professional Carwashing & Detailing* magazine, some car washes are adding pet washes thanks to PetClin®, a do-it-yourself doggie wash machine. Honest! (See www.petclin.com.) Now, we're not saying you necessarily want people washing their dogs at your car wash, but the point is that there are a whole host of services you can provide that you may not have thought of. Kids' rides are easy to manage and another way to make money while the kids wait with their parents. These are the ones where 50 cents or even a dollar starts the horse, racing car, or other ride. The bottom line is that there are numerous options for additional income.

Numbers Talk

How much will you earn as a car wash owner? The numbers here vary greatly depending on a number of factors, including the size of your facility and your location. Here are some ballpark numbers to give you a rough idea of what to expect:

○ *Self-service*   average monthly gross income a bay = $1,200 to $1,700

○ *In-bay automatic*   average monthly gross income a bay = $3,500 to $4,500

○ *Exterior-conveyor*   average monthly gross income = $25,000 to $45,000

○ *Full-service*   average monthly gross income = $50,000 to $75,000

Taken together, extras such as vacuums, vending machines, carpet and upholstery cleaning, snack shops, dog washing, and similar services and products can dramatically boost your bottom line. How much? The average full-service wash takes in an additional $18,000 every month from non-wash sales. Exterior-conveyor washes make about an extra $7,000 a month. For self-service facilities, vacuums bring in about $1,000 a month, carpet and upholstery cleaning around $100, air fresheners about $200, and soda and snack sales, $250.

> ## Smart Tip — Tip...
> Offering a spot-free rinse cycle at your self-service wash may be a good idea. Not only will it make your customers happier by leaving cars looking better, it can also increase your revenue because customers will generally buy more time to use the feature.

Other Automotive Services

Although we're not going to get too far into the subject in this book, there are some other services you can provide if you have the space. Detailing is a logical extension for some car washes, as are quickie oil and lube jobs. Here are some basic considerations that will determine if these services are appropriate for your wash.

- *Space.* Land is expensive. In fact, it'll probably cost you nearly as much to obtain the land for your wash as it will to equip the wash itself. Therefore, it could very well be that adding major offline services is simply cost-prohibitive. If you do have land available for more services, you might want to think about whether that space would better be used for additional wash services—more self-service bays, an in-bay automatic unit, or extra vacuum islands in the case of a full-service wash.

- *Expertise.* Learning the car wash business is hard enough without having to learn about everything that goes into performing other automotive services as well. If you're going to have your hands full learning the ins and outs of running a car wash on a day-to-day basis, you might want to think about whether you're going to have the time or the inclination to perform these additional services properly.

- *Employees.* If you're operating a self-service wash and don't plan on hiring any employees, you should realize that by adding additional services such as those mentioned above, you'll almost certainly need to hire workers. If one of the things that attracted you to the car wash business in the first place was that you didn't need to worry about employees and the hassle that goes along with them, you probably aren't going to want to hire employees for services that that aren't part of your core business anyway.

- *Demand.* Is there a demand for the extra services you want to provide? When you were scouting possible locations for your car wash, you took into account lots of information. One element was competition. You'll now have to go through that process again to determine if there's enough demand and a sufficient lack of competition in your area for the extra services you're considering.

Should You Lease Your Extra Space?

We've already talked about the need to have adequate space for the type of wash you want to construct, but what if, after you do all of your analysis and build a wash the community will support, you are in the enviable position of having too much space? There are any number of things you can do—build a small store, add vacuum islands, etc. But another option is to lease the space to someone else.

For example, what if your research indicates that a quick lube, oil change, or detailing service is in demand in your area, but you don't want to run it? It might be possible for you to rent the space to someone who does want to run it. Some owners have done just that. If you're serious about trying it, you can make an attempt to raid a local Jiffy-Lube or similar outfit for an experienced manager to run it—someone who lacks the resources to go into business for himself.

You can work out the financial details in a number of different ways. One way would be to lease the space outright. This is a good idea if you're looking for a steady stream of income every month, no matter how much business your new partner does. You could also structure the agreement so that the tenant simply keeps a percentage of revenue. The disadvantage to this type of arrangement is that you don't know from one month to the next what you're going to take in.

Another idea is to rent out the space as a storage place or small warehouse. Depending on the amount of land you have available and existing structures that may already be on it, you could lease it to a small auto-repair shop or inspection station.

Whatever you decide, there's simply no reason to allow extra land to go to waste, especially not when there are so many possibilities. Just make sure you lease to tenants you can trust, and make sure you do not create a log-jam problem with cars blocking up your entrances or exits. Think through the logistics very carefully before leasing to another consumer business.

Financial Management

You knew it had to come to this. Yes, you are going to have to spend some time sitting behind a desk and filling out paperwork or hiring someone to do it for you. In the long run, it's going to be very hard for you to succeed without a solid financial plan. Set up some sort of system to track your revenue and expenditures. This can be as low-tech as a notebook or as high-tech as sophisticated accounting software. Whatever works best for you is fine.

At least once every month, sit down and figure out all your income and expenses for the previous period, and have your accountant's phone number on hand so she can answer questions or come in and review the finances with you. This may be a bit more important for a car wash owner than for someone in a business where most money is received by check or credit card. If you're in

Stat Fact

The average owner of an exterior-conveyor or full-service car wash loses $2,500 to theft in a year, according to *Professional Carwashing & Detailing* magazine.

that type of business, you might be able to let things slide a bit and reconstruct these numbers based on receipts and statements. But for a car wash owner, someone who's emptying a register (or change machine) every day, keeping a close watch on everything that goes in and out the door is critical.

We discussed the role a good accountant can play in Chapter 5, and it may very well be that hiring one is going to be the best thing for you. If the cost is prohibitive, then consider that your time is also a valuable commodity. Every hour that you spend recording every little detail in a financial ledger is one less hour you have to grow your business.

An accountant can also assist you should you run into any problems with the IRS. No one likes to think about the possibility of being audited, but it certainly does happen. If your books have been professionally maintained, you're probably going to lower the risk of overlooking something important that might result in fines and additional taxes.

This is also an important reason to maintain records from previous years, but certainly not the only one. After all, you can't chart the growth of your business if you aren't tracking its performance over time. You could do this on your own (millions of individual taxpayers already do), but again, an accountant may be able to help you set up a system that's more efficient.

In addition to the legal reasons you want to keep accurate books, there's also a business reason for it. A good system will allow you to see where your business is strong and where it needs some help. It can help you determine if a new profit center is actually adding to your bottom line or just eating up precious resources. It can also help you identify areas where you might be able to cut costs.

Stat Fact

According to a recent survey by *Professional Carwashing & Detailing* magazine, only 37 percent of self-service car wash owners derive their primary source of income from their car wash business.

Dealing with Taxes

Death and taxes are two things you can always count on. Another reason for keeping accurate account of your finances will come on April 15 of every year. In addition to paying your federal taxes, you're going to have to pay state and local taxes as well. Add to those taxes, the taxes you're going to have to pay regularly for your employees, and you've got a potential mess on your hands.

If you can afford it, it probably makes sense to hire an accountant to handle your taxes for you. The tax process for a business can be a real maze, especially if you have employees. An accountant should be able to make sure you do it right and haven't left yourself exposed to penalties because you forgot to make a payment here and there.

The laws are always changing, and an accountant can help you figure out things such as depreciation and other legitimate business expenses that most laymen simply won't know about. Plus, hiring someone to handle this for you frees up your time for more important things—like dreaming up that new marketing plan. In the next chapter, we'll look into the ins and outs of marketing and advertising for your car wash business.

Advertising, Marketing, and Public Relations

Most of the decisions that you make that will affect your chances for success in the car wash business are probably going to be made before you ever set up shop: location, type of wash, equipment purchases, mission statement, philosophy, etc. How you market your new business and how you handle public relations are two very important factors that will determine your ongoing success once you open your doors (or turn on the faucets, as the case may be).

You basically have three ways you can differentiate yourself from your competition. You can compete on price, you can compete on services and amenities, and/or you can market yourself better than anyone else. You'll most likely be doing all three of those things, but marketing yourself well is one of the least expensive ways to increase both volume and revenue.

Creating a Marketing Plan

The one thing that's important to remember before you get started is that, no matter which type of car wash you decide to open, you're going to be targeting specific customers. As we've mentioned earlier, a self-service car wash is generally going to attract customers in a lower income bracket than a full-service operation. Common to all car wash owners is the fact that home washers represent a significant segment of the untapped market for your services. Remember, according to the International Carwash Association (ICA), about 50 percent of the population still chooses to wash their cars at home. When you come up with your marketing plan, focus some of your energy on how to convince those home washers to abandon their hose and bucket, and turn the task over to a professional.

Direct Mail

The purpose of any marketing campaign is to increase awareness for your business among the people most likely to use your services. Direct mail can work in a number of different ways and draw in customers who might otherwise not be driving by your wash. One way of direct marketing is joining in a larger coupon mailing with other area businesses, thus sharing the cost of the mailing. Another option is to purchase a mailing list on your own. However, you need to make sure the list is current.

Larger mailing lists: Just about every community is served by a company that does massive bulk mailing of coupons for businesses in the area. You've probably received these mailings yourself. Typically, they'll come in a large envelope and contain maybe two dozen coupons for everything from eyeglasses to movie rentals. Why not try adding some coupons for your car wash? This does two things right away. First, it captures those people who are not yet aware of your business. Second, if some of the people receiving the mailing normally visit another wash, a coupon from you might be just the thing that makes them change their buying habits and visit your wash instead. You should check with your local chamber of commerce or other business owners for recommendations on coupon companies that have had success serving your area. Again, be very careful that the list is not dated—an old list will have a high percentage of people or businesses that are no longer at the addresses listed.

The second type of direct mail is going to require quite a bit more work on your part. This involves renting or buying mailing lists that you use on your own to contact potential customers in your area. For this to be effective, you should already have a good idea of some demographic criteria of you recipients. For instance, perhaps you'd like to reach all registered owners of vehicles in a particular zip code who rent, rather than own, their own home. Maybe you'd like to reach those people who have purchased a new car within the past six months or people who fall into a particular income bracket. Whatever the criteria, start to develop some general guidelines for just what type of customer you'll be trying to reach before you move on to the next step.

The next thing you're going to want to do is to find a good mailing-list broker. You can search on the internet, look in the Yellow Pages, or contact a group such as the Direct Marketing Association (www.thedma.org) that should be able to provide you with some leads.

A good broker is crucial to your success in any direct-mail effort, so spend some time evaluating your options before deciding with which one to work. Direct mail isn't cheap, so it's important that you get the most bang for your buck. You'll probably pay anywhere from $20 to $100 for 1,000 names on a list, depending how targeted the list is, who's offering it, and the format in which it's delivered (the price generally goes up if you get the list on mail-ready labels). Check out www.listsnow.com on the internet to get a general idea of what's available and what it will cost.

Theme Schemes

Theme washes can take many forms, and depending on how extensively you want to outfit your site, it can get very expensive. Some theme washes can easily run well over $2 million to build.

Of course, there are cheaper alternatives. Some owners have tried creating haunted car washes with a few strobe lights, maybe a fog machine, and some employees to volunteer to put on a monster show for customers. It might be something to think about during the Halloween season to draw in additional customers. The equipment you would need for a haunted car wash isn't really that extensive or expensive. Owners who have tried it say that customers generally get a kick out of it, and parents especially enjoy bringing children for the experience. With a little ingenuity, you can come up with a space travel theme or any number of unique possibilities. As long as it does not interfere with the customer getting a quality wash, a theme can be worthwhile, if it is not cost prohibitive.

▲

What are some of the services that a good broker will be able to provide? For starters, one will be to narrow your universe of names and addresses down to only those specific types of people you've identified as being good targets for a direct-mail campaign. For example, corporate CEOs probably aren't the best targets for coupons to a self-service car wash. If you're mailing to the wrong types of people, you're simply wasting money. Second, a good broker will be able to work with you to come up with ideas you may not have thought of. In other words, you're going to have a general idea of who you want to reach, but the specifics of how to achieve that level of targeting may best be left to the true professionals.

In addition to brokers, there are other sources of mailing lists you may want to consider. Think about where your customers, or potential customers, might "cross over" with other businesses in your area, and see if you can strike a deal to obtain their mailing list. It certainly can't hurt to ask. For example, it may be possible to rent or buy mailing lists from local car dealerships, with names and addresses of people who have purchased a new or used car in the past month. You may pay a bit more for a contact by going this route, rather than through a list broker, but it might be worth it for such a highly targeted list.

Another thing to consider when you're marketing through direct mail is that it might be a smart idea to be a bit creative about your offerings. For example, instead of simply providing a blanket coupon that covers all times and days of the week, perhaps you may want to offer a midweek special or a similar offer that draws people to your wash during your slower periods.

Also, design your coupons to stand out among a sea of coupons that people typically receive. A catchy phrase, a unique color (just make sure the print is still legible), or a clever design can make people notice your coupon.

Distributing Fliers

This type of marketing requires a bit more legwork, but it can be a lot cheaper than paying to obtain mailing lists. Fliers under the windshield wipers of your car, on your doorknob at home, or in your mailbox are common in most communities. They tout everything from a home contractor to a new pizzeria. Why not put that method to use for your car wash?

You can try this in a number of different ways. For instance, if there's a local mall or some other location where a large number of

> **Smart Tip**
>
> Having trouble thinking about new ways to build business at your wash? Try visiting your competitors as a customer to see if they're doing anything new or innovative. While you don't want to copy them, you could get some novel ideas. Also, look at what other service businesses are doing. Perhaps you can translate an idea from a nearby restaurant or repair shop and use it in your marketing.

cars park, you can try placing fliers on cars, offering discounted washes for one day only, for a week, or whatever you decide. You can also try leaving a stack in the lobby of a large apartment building near your business, with permission of the management (otherwise they'll be tossed in the garbage). Wherever there are people with cars—especially if they don't have adequate space or resources to wash them on their own—there's an opportunity for you to grow your business. Take advantage of it.

One of the drawbacks to this technique is that someone, and it probably isn't going to be you, has to go out and physically distribute the fliers. If you're the trusting sort, you might be comfortable simply handing a stack of fliers to one of your employees and assuming that they'll do the job correctly. However, if you think you might need to add a little extra incentive, there are some simple ways to do just that. What about letting your employee know that for every customer who comes in with one of those fliers, the employee will receive a certain percentage of the sale or a flat rate for each car. It doesn't have to be much, just enough to keep them from walking a block or two down the street, dumping the fliers in a garbage can, and taking the rest of the day off. If you make it lucrative enough, you might just find that your employees will jump at the chance to be the "man on the street," rather than viewing it as a chore they'd rather push off on someone else. The other option is hiring high school or college students to do the job.

Again, the flier needs to be designed in a way that grabs people's attention. Color, bold print, a clever design, a catch phrase, anything that stands out (tastefully) could make the difference between having your fliers tossed or held onto. Hint: Don't put too

In the Know

Let's imagine this scenario. You just purchased a four-bay, self-service wash that has been in the community for years. You decide to convert one of the self-service bays into an in-bay automatic unit, but after a few weeks, you're disappointed to find that the automatic unit isn't bringing in the kind of business you had hoped. What's the problem? It could be that your customers don't know it's there.

The solution? Make sure your customers know about all your facilities. Paint arrows on your lot directing them to the automatic bay. Put signs in and around your bays advertising all the choices you're offering. Do this with any detailing services you may offer as well. Put signs in your bays that let people know where your vacuuming islands are, for example. It's a small expense that can make a big difference in your bottom line.

much on the page or it will look cluttered and get tossed. Think of it as if someone had just handed it to you. Would the flier grab your attention? Would you read it? Is it too wordy? Is it unclear? Look at the flier as if you were seeing it for the first time.

For distribution, you can could also work a deal with a local newspaper to insert the fliers into their paper and even provide employees of the paper with a free wash for doing so.

Database Marketing

This type of marketing requires ongoing work on your part, as well as some knowledge of computers, to be done right. If you're going to be putting a significant amount of effort into the project, you're going to want a significant return—and according to many car wash experts, you'll get it.

So how does it work? Basically, database marketing is used to track individual customers or groups of customers, allowing you to monitor what they buy and when they buy it. As mentioned earlier, there are car wash specific software programs from DRB, Innovative Control Systems Inc., and Integrated Systems Inc. that monitor the car wash and count the volume of cars and what services drivers utilized. Of course, you can also buy any general database package available. Microsoft Access is one example and you can check Apple for Mac data management programs as well. However, you will need one of your employees to record all of the data. The key here is to be as accurate and specific as possible. You want more than just a name for each customer. Ideally, you'd like to include the name, mailing address, type of car they drive, and the package they order each time they visit your wash. There may be other pieces of information you'd like to know, but this is pretty much the minimum of what you'll need to make database marketing worthwhile.

It's all well and good to say that's the information you want to collect. But how do you go about collecting it? This is a total team effort. Someone is going to have to record the information initially and then pass it along to the person who will be doing the actual data entry. Who collects this information is up to you; perhaps it will be your cashier or your service writer.

To capture names and contact information initially, it might be a good idea to use one of the other marketing tactics we'll discuss—such as a frequent-buyer program—to get customers to give you that information initially. You can also try running some sort of contest or raffle, where customers fill out a card with their name and address, or simply drop off their business card. Maybe you could give away one free deluxe wash or even a coupon book good for several washes if you want to increase the chances that people will take the time to give you their information.

Once you've gathered this information, you can use it in several ways. First, as an auto mechanic might do, you can use the information to determine when a regular

Some E-Mail Tips

Make sure the "from" line is the name of the car wash. Too many business owners use their name or some other name in the from line and customers delete the e-mail immediately because they don't know what it is. Also, if you are sending out e-mails, make sure the part that shows up in most preview windows is an attention grabber, since that's what people see when scanning their e-mails and deleting those that they did not expect. Remember, you have two seconds in which to grab the person's attention before he or she hits delete.

Second, you can get a sense of what types of customers buy what types of wash packages. You can use this information to try to convert a habitual exterior-only customer into a full-service customer. For example, say you notice that you have 500 regular customers who come in once a month for an exterior wash and have never opted for your deluxe package. What do you think would happen if you sent each of those customers a coupon for a free upgrade to a deluxe wash when they purchase their standard exterior-only package? The first result, which is almost definite, is that it will build customer loyalty. After all, you know them well enough to anticipate their car washing needs even before they do. But more important, what might also wind up happening is that the customer sees what a terrific deal the deluxe wash is and becomes a regular deluxe wash buyer. It's almost like saying to the customer, "Let me show you what a really great wash makes your car look like. If you don't think it's worth it, then by all means we'd still love to serve you with our standard service." What you're doing is introducing them to something they've never tried before in the hopes that they'll become hooked.

Database marketing can also help you if you decide to embark on a direct-mail campaign that will require you to rent lists. By studying your own customer data, you'll probably be able to spot trends or buying patterns among similar groups of people. Using this information, you can assume that others (who aren't your customers) who share those characteristics might tend to buy the same type of product or service. Then, when you start combing through the mailing lists available, or working with a broker, you can be a bit more specific in terms of the characteristics you're looking for in the list. As we said earlier, direct mail isn't cheap, so any way you can find to increase your rate of response is going to be a big help.

▲

Smart Tip

Tip...

Marketing isn't a one-size-fits-all science. Some approaches may work best with one group (advertising in supermarkets for stay-at-home moms, for example), but not with others. When deciding on the best methods to reach new customers, you should think about who you're trying to attract, based on your community's demographics and the services you provide.

customer might be due for a certain type of service—the same way the mechanic might contact a customer when it's time for an oil change. Dropping a quick postcard in the mail costs you virtually nothing, and if it can increase the frequency at which your customers come in, it can be well worth it. Also, make sure to get e-mail addresses. As long as customers give you their e-mail and permission to contact them, you won't be sending SPAM, (illegal junk mail). Instead you can send e-mail reminders, which is very quick and cost effective. Add in a coupon or discount and people won't delete your offer quite so fast. Today, millions of people communicate largely through e-mail, so if you can reach people via e-communications, why not do so as long as you don't become a pest.

Utilizing the Internet

It's nearly impossible today to find a business that does not have some internet presence. That means that even if you do not have your own web site, you still want to be listed in local online directories, on the chamber of commerce site (usually you need only to join) and in local business listings. You may elect to advertise on a popular local site as well. If you do opt for your own site, you can usually do a domain search and get a site up and running inexpensively through any number of companies. Hiring someone to build a site isn't difficult; you will find local site designers in all parts of the country. The key is to look at some of the sites they have designed and pick a design that you think will work for your business.

If you do opt for a web site, it is for promotional purposes and to market your wash. The site for a car wash is typically one to three pages, explaining the different types of washes offered, the prices, and perhaps some discounts. Basically, the site should be simple, meaning avoid the bells and whistles—like fancy graphics. Have easy to read, but not in-your-face, wording and some photos, if possible.

As mentioned earlier, you can also use permission-based e-mail marketing, whereby someone gives you permission to e-mail them, and you send clever reminders once a month or thereabouts. This can also be a way of launching a contest or promoting a special holiday theme, such as a haunted wash for Halloween. Also, think in terms of spreading the word by having something worth forwarding to a friend. Perhaps you'll add in a great car care tip with a forward-to-a-friend link so that your recipient can share the tip with friends. Naturally it will say this tip is courtesy of your car wash. Try a two-for-one discount so if a friend shows up with your regular customer, he or she will also benefit from your promotional discount.

If you're running a large conveyor wash, you could even consider an e-mail newsletter, where once a month, or every other month, you send a short online newsletter to all who have signed up to receive such discounts. However, even sending a discount can get boring to the recipient if it's essentially the same, or very similar, every time. Therefore, hook them into reading it with a little bit of content in the form of two or three paragraphs on car care each month. Surround your content with plenty of offers, promotion, photos, and perhaps even a contest. E-mail newsletters can be very effective, provided you keep them interesting. Also make sure the recipient knows it's from your business by using the same "from" name each time. They won't know your name, but they will know the name of the car wash and won't delete it if there's something of interest to read.

Otherwise, keep the web site up to date. Change the promotions and discounts, and make note of any charity events you have run or are planning in the future. If you sponsor a local baseball team, mention that on the web site (and even post a team photo), and you'll have the parents of each kid on the team using your wash. Make the site informative and clever.

Along with having a web site, you need to promote the site so that people will know it's there. To do so, you need to have the web address on everything, from receipts to the bags you use in the shop portion of your wash.

The other important aspect of web promotion is cross-promotion with other businesses. Trade ads with a local business, putting a mention of their business—and a link to their web site—on your web site in exchange for an ad on their site and a link to your web site. This way, you draw from their customer base as well. Naturally, you'll want to think about the best demographic audience. For example, you might trade ads and links with an auto repair business or even a used car dealership.

Exterior Signage

Your best marketing tool just may be your signage. To understand why, think of it this way: A car wash is a unique business. In some ways, it's like the impulse racks at supermarket checkouts. Many of your customers will simply pull into your wash on an impulse. It's those impulse customers, the ones who don't have a regular schedule for when they wash their cars, that you want to attract. They may realize that their car needs a wash for a week, two weeks, or even months before they ever get it done. If they happen to be out, have some free time, and spot a wash, they'll pull in. These are the customers you need to reach with your signs. Your business will most likely depend on it.

What makes a good sign? Let's talk about your main sign first—the one that's designed to be seen from the street while motorists drive by at whatever rate of speed is typical for your location. This means being tall enough and big enough to be seen clearly. It also needs to be eye-catching. Keep in mind that to some degree your signage choices may be limited by local zoning regulations.

Nevertheless, in terms of what goes on the sign itself, there's really only one major rule. The words "car wash" need to be the biggest thing on the sign. If you want to decorate it with bubbles or soapsuds, fine. A picture of a shiny, freshly washed and waxed sports car? Great. As long as the words "car wash" are the first and most prominent thing a driver sees, you're in business. As mentioned earlier, test out the viewing potential of the sign, which should be readable from 300 feet away, and easy to view from several angles. Also make sure the sign is not blocked by other signs, businesses, or by trees. Remember, signs can only be read in a split second by a driver, so limit the wording to the name of the wash, where it is located, and the type of wash—if that's not clear by the name.

Micky's Soft Brush Car Wash – Turn 300 Feet!!

Jesse's Car Wash: Full Service – Next Left

Interior Signage

By interior signage, what we're really talking about are the signs that your customers see once they pull into your property. Of the variety of signs you'll probably have posted,

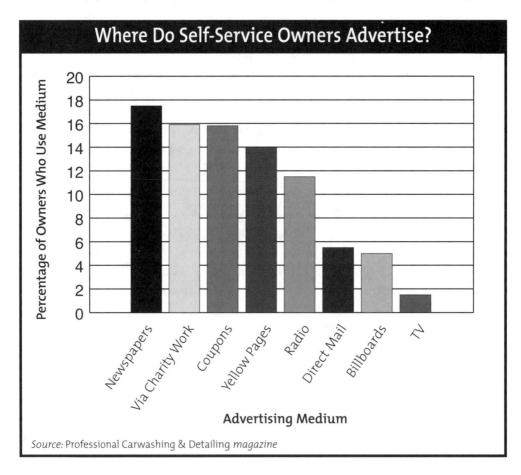

Source: Professional Carwashing & Detailing magazine

perhaps the most important is your menu of services. This is your bill of fare, the choices or various levels of service you're offering to your customers. Why is this so important? Think about a restaurant. You want choices. You want choices in terms of the variety of food, and you want choices in terms of price. Car wash customers are not going to be any different. If they want a full-service wash, wax, vacuum, etc., they want to have it available to them. If, on the other hand, they only want a simple and quick exterior cleaning, they aren't going to want to be forced into paying more for services they don't want or feel they need.

While this level of choice isn't going to apply (at least to the same extent) for a self-service wash, for most other types of washes, chances are you're going to be offering numerous levels of service. Your menu of services plays a vital role in marketing your car wash.

Product Sales and Placement

If you choose to sell other products, either in a separate gift shop or in vending machines located in your wash bays or somewhere else on your property, you'll want to think about the best place to position whatever it is you're going to be selling. If you're selling from a separate gift store, the location will probably be determined by where you have space for the facility. For vending machines, it's a little bit different. You're probably going to have a much wider range of options. If you have vacuuming facilities, this might not be a bad place to locate your vending machines. Near a change machine is another good option, because you don't want customers to have to search for a place to spend their money once they have it in their hands. Either of these locations will make it easy for your customers to make an impulse buy with any extra change they have left over once they're done with their wash.

If you're operating a tunnel wash, it's not a bad idea to have some vending machines and other products in the area where the customers walk through or wait, assuming, of course, that the customers actually leave their car during the wash process. If the customers do stay in the car, you'll probably want to locate the machines in an area where customers are likely to get out of their cars, such as a vacuum island. Try to determine the most logical place in which to put sales items so that your customers can easily find them.

Media Advertising

The high cost of advertising on television puts this avenue out of reach for most new car wash owners, unless you can strike a deal with a local cable channel. But there are other media outlets that you might want to explore. Newspapers can be a good place to

> **Stat Fact**
> Half of exterior-conveyor owners and 60 percent of full-service owners post signs explaining the wash process, and 44 percent even post reprints of articles about car washing, according to the International Carwash Association.

try, especially local weeklies because the cost is usually much lower than with the major daily papers.

You can also try finding newsletters or other publications that cater to a local audience. Is there a large apartment community nearby? Chances are it publishes a newsletter that is distributed to residents, probably once a month. These are your prime customers—those without the space or resources to wash their own cars—so tapping into publications such as these can be a great idea. Your best bet is to contact apartment managers in your area to see if such publications exist and whether or not they accept advertising.

Let the Truth Be Known

There are many things about car washes your customers probably believe that will tend to keep them away from your business. How much do you think it would cost to print a few hundred fliers that make the true facts known? If you're doing it from your own computer and your own printer, it'll cost next to nothing. For example, squelching the myth that car washes are bad for the environment—in an age of environmental concern—could be beneficial for your business and help you draw some of the driveway car washers.

It's easy to understand how this myth got started. Take a trip through any car wash tunnel and what do you see? Torrents of water. Not only that, but all the water that's being used is presumably directed to the sewer system—sludge, grease, dirt, and all. Certainly, this can't be good for the environment. That's what most customers probably think, but it's not true.

Most car washes use a water reclamation system that recycles a great deal of the water used in the wash process. Some of these systems can reclaim close to 100 percent of the water used, saving fresh water for rinse cycles only. And there's more: The high-pressure wash systems at professional car washes are designed to do more with less. In other words, they can do a better job at cleaning cars with less water than anything you could do at home. When the typical home washer cleans his car in the driveway, he's using anywhere from 80 to 140 gallons of water every ten minutes. At a professional car wash, a typical wash-and-rinse cycle uses between 8 and 45 gallons, depending on the type of equipment used.

Consider posting a sign that encapsulates this information so that all your customers see it when they enter your wash. Boast about your equipment. Let people know that your water is reclaimed. Position yourself as an environmentally friendly car wash. You can also post this information on your web site.

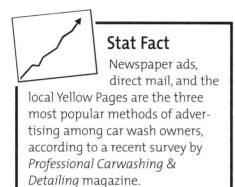

Yellow Pages and Print Ads

Yellow Page advertising is important for most businesses. It allows you to stand out when someone is thumbing through the book, so inquire about pricing in local Yellow Page directories. Make sure you proof the ad carefully before sending it, because you're stuck with it for a year. For online Yellow Page directories, you should also proof your ad, but at least it can be changed if there's an error or a typo. Look into all local online Yellow Page advertising.

Also consider other places where you see print ads, including posters on construction sites, ads on the side of local busses, and even placemat ads at the local eateries. All of these are places to put your name. Inquire about costs and stay within your advertising budget. Wherever possible, work barter deals, for example, taxis often have ads on the roof of the cab. Perhaps you could wash x number of cabs at an off hour each month in exchange for your ads on the roof of the cabs.

Word-of-Mouth Advertising

While all the techniques we've discussed so far can be helpful, there's also a form of advertising that you can't buy—at least not directly. Word-of-mouth advertising is very important to a neighborhood business such as a car wash. Nothing beats one neighbor telling another that a new restaurant, new store, or new car wash is a great place to take your business.

Traditional advertising that you pay for can help bring customers to your shop initially, but once they get there, you have to continue to deliver—through quality services, friendly employees, and fair prices—so that they, in turn, will turn into advertisers for you.

Special Promotions

Many, many companies use what are called premiums to attract or retain customers. America Online once gave away books as part of a retention premium—a gift designed to encourage customers to renew their subscription to the service. The gift was a book that retailed for about $10. In truth, America Online probably bought the books for around $3 or $4 each. It's a simple equation. If you spend $3 to keep a customer who's going to wind up spending at least $200 over the course of the year, isn't that worth it?

You can give away a free book of coupons or other promotional items that spread the word about your car wash. There are numerous possibilities from decals, stickers, and car-related items to caps, pens, and, of course, t-shirts.

Special promotional days or events can also draw customers. Have a free donut day or give away hot dogs one day at lunchtime. Low cost but fun items that draw people in (with big signs out front) more than pay for themselves. Promote such days on your web site.

Premium Deals

Consider which companies or organizations out there would like to give away books of coupons for free car washes to their members or customers. There are probably dozens of them. Some might include local car clubs, new or used car dealerships, churches, and a host of charitable organizations.

Bear in mind that you aren't giving away anything. The way a premium deal works is that the company or organization buys the coupon books from you, and they in turn give them away to their members or customers. The best part, depending on how you look at it, is that this is money that you're going to make whether or not the final recipients of the coupons ever use them. In other words, you may make money for washing cars that you may never actually wash. It doesn't get much better than that.

So, how should you go about approaching these organizations? The first message you must convey is that your coupon books will provide some sort of value to the eventual recipient. For example, have you ever heard ads for car dealerships that offer $100 worth of free gas with any new or used car purchase? They're doing it simply because it's an added incentive for a customer to make a purchase from that dealership, rather than from one down the road offering a similar price on a similar car. This can work the same way with a book of 10 or 20 coupons for a free car wash. The dealerships buy the books from you, and then offer them as an added bonus when salespeople are trying to close the deal.

The same holds true for other organizations. Banks, for example, are famous for giving away items such as calendars every year. But while many people probably just throw out a calendar, there's a much greater chance that they'll hold onto a book full of coupons for a free car wash because this represents a real value. This is the message you want to get across to whatever organization you approach: the gift is going to mean something.

The second point you want to stress is that the customer will remember and associate the gift with the company or organization that gave it to them. Help them along with this by offering to customize the product. You might offer free customization to any "bulk buyer" who purchases more than 100 coupon books, for example. All you have to

Stat Fact

Nearly 50 percent of self-service owners don't advertise at all, according to a recent survey by *Professional Carwashing & Detailing* magazine. Lower prices (and thus lower revenue from each customer) probably make it cost-prohibitive.

do is print the company's name (or some other message of their choosing) alongside your own in the coupon book. You might also want to try offering discounts to companies that buy a large quantity.

One-Day-Only Specials

If you anticipate that traffic is going to be particularly slow on a certain day, you might try jazzing it up a bit by running a one-day-

only special—maybe a discounted wash or a free add-on service. You can also try running midweek specials. Many establishments, such as dry cleaners, run specials on clothes brought in during the week, as opposed to those dropped off on a Saturday or Sunday. Because the weekend is most likely going to be your busiest time, try reducing your price slightly or adding services for those days of the week when you notice that your traffic flow slacks a bit. The beauty of this type of promotion is that it adds a sense of urgency. A driver on the fence, wavering between getting his car washed and waiting another couple of weeks, might just decide now is the time if he really wants to take advantage of the special you're running. As mentioned above, Mike G. from Carson City, California, uses midweek specials on his slowest days to attract more customers.

Holiday specials are another option and can be anything you want them to be. Run a Mother's Day special, where moms get a reduced-price wash. If customers come to expect these types of promotions, it can also help to build a base of regulars who choose your wash over another because they know they're always going to get a better value from you. Today it might be a free wax application, tomorrow it might be a free vacuum; it doesn't matter. Whatever it is, it's more than what the guy down the street is offering.

Frequent-Buyer Programs

In the car wash business, loyalty is very important. Because the services you're going to provide is very similar to the competition, you're going to need to find a way to differentiate yourself. A frequent-buyer promotion might be just the ticket.

You've probably seen these promotions in a variety of different businesses, including car washes. Customers receive a card (usually business card size to fit into the wallet) with ten numbers, in boxes, around the perimeter. Each time the customer returns and has his or her car washed, the cashier punches out one of the squares with a hole puncher or marks it with a special stamp. When all the squares are gone or marked, the customer receives a free car wash. Hint: mark it or punch it in a unique shape so that the customer can't go home and punch out or mark them all him- or herself.

Tip...

Smart Tip

Build customer loyalty by being around your wash as much as possible and making a point to remember your frequent customers. If you own a self-service wash, every third or fourth wash, give them a free wash to say thanks. Almost nothing makes customers feel better than to know the owner appreciates their business.

Cross-Merchandising

Let's say your wash is located a block away from a gas station or convenience store. Assuming these establishments aren't offering, and don't plan to offer, car washing services, they represent a prime target for a cross-merchandising opportunity. Your goal here is to use their store or station to drive customers to your wash. This can be accomplished in a number of ways. The most popular is to have the store give their customers coupons for a discounted wash (perhaps $1 or $2 off the regular wash price) when they buy a certain amount of goods.

It may seem odd at first for an unrelated store to help you promote your business for free. After all, it's not like you're going to be offering $1 off a gas purchase with the purchase of a deluxe wash. But when you think about it, you begin to see that the store is getting something out of the arrangement as well. If the offer is for a discounted wash when the customer buys a certain amount—$10 worth of a gas or a fill-up, for example—you're helping the store increase the average purchase from each customer. It wouldn't make sense for the other business not to agree to help you out.

Sponsorship

Your car wash name on the uniforms of a local little league team, or sponsoring a local community theater production and being listed in the show's program, is a great way to show community support and keep your name in front of the public. Why won't the parents of each kid on that little league team come to your car wash when their cars are in need of a cleaning? After all, they see the name every time they watch their kids play. Sponsorship puts you in a favorable light in the community.

The Grand Opening

The day the cars start rolling into your wash isn't just important because you'll finally start seeing a return on your investment. It's also important because this is when you get your first, and perhaps best, chance to hype your wash to the hilt.

The goal with any grand opening is to create, for lack of a better word, a spectacle. You want people to pay attention. You want drivers to stop. You even want pedestrians to take a look at what's going on (they probably have cars, too). One car wash consulting company rents a giant inflatable turtle to help draw customers to their clients' grand openings. That's certainly a start. Surely you're going to want to have flags flapping in the wind and balloons to hand out to all neighborhood kids. Depending on your location, you might also be able to put employees with signs along the sidewalk (as long as they aren't in danger of being struck by passing cars). The bottom line is that you don't want to rule anything out that you think might work.

In terms of specifically what you can do during your grand opening, it's pretty wide open. To help you think of some ideas, try to remember the last grand opening you saw for a store that caught your attention. Think specifically about what attracted you to the location. This may give you some idea of things you can try with your own car wash.

Give a good deal of thought to the timing of your grand opening. Remember the statistics about when most washes do their best business. To generalize, you can probably say that a sunny Saturday morning or an afternoon in the cold winter months are going to be your busiest times. It may seem like this would be a great time for a grand opening. However, if you are new to the car wash business, you might want to open on a more quiet weekday, giving yourself a few days before the first "big weekend" to iron out any kinks in the system.

Remember, your grand opening doesn't have to be on just one day either. It could conceivably last for an entire week, or even an entire month. It might be best for you to open in the middle of the week, get at least a feel for what you can expect and for some of the issues you're going to have to deal with on a daily basis, and then tackle the weekend crowds.

Let's say you designate the month of February as your grand opening period. During the first week, maybe you can offer half-price washes. During the second week, maybe you can offer a free upgrade to your best wash at the regular wash price. For the third week, maybe you could offer a coupon for a free or discounted wash during the customer's next visit. For the fourth week, perhaps you could offer discounted coupon books good for five or ten washes over a certain period of time. Those are just some suggestions, but you can see how extending the grand opening period allows you to make more of an impact on the car wash customer. Not only will you capture people who don't happen to drive by your wash every day, you'll also give yourself the opportunity to turn those occasional customers into regulars by offering them a reason to come back.

Bright Idea

Offer insurance for your customers. No, not health insurance or automotive insurance, but rain insurance. Guarantee that if it rains less than 24 hours after they wash their car, you'll wash it again for free when they show you their receipt. This can help boost business on days when people might hold off getting a wash because of poor weather reports.

Charity Partnerships

Hosting a car wash is a tried-and-true method for many charities—especially schools and academically related clubs and teams—to raise money for their cause. Oftentimes, a charity event will be held in a parking lot or similar venue on school grounds, where the kids will normally wash and dry cars using handheld sponges and buckets of soapy water. How do you think the kids would feel about having the use of your car wash for a day? No, you're not going to turn over the keys to the shop. But you can arrange to donate part of your revenue from that day to their cause.

Exactly what formula you use is up to you. Maybe you simply donate a percentage of your revenue, a specific amount for each car washed above what your normal volume would be on that day, or some other arrangement you come up with.

A car wash-charity partnership shows goodwill in your community. While this isn't something you can put a price tag on, it shows you in a very positive light. Remember, the vast majority of your customers are going to come from within three or four miles of your location. You are very much tied to the community in which your car wash lies.

You are also getting your own personal public relations squad for free. Instead of the band members promoting a car wash they held on their own in some vacant parking lot, they'll now be promoting your car wash. There's no doubt they'll be doing some PR campaigning before the event by encouraging supporters to show up, but you should also ask them to come to your business on the big day to help pull in passersby.

Finally, you have a chance of getting free publicity, such as in the local paper that covers the charity event and mentions your car wash in print—a free ad! Not bad.

Customer Relations

As we've mentioned, one of the keys to running a successful car wash business over the long haul is customer service. People simply won't come back if they feel they haven't been treated properly. If you're on-site during the hours of operation, as you most likely will be if you operate any kind of conveyor wash, you'll have ample opportunity to take care of your customers. For owners of self-service washes, this task will be more challenging. They'll have to be a bit more creative in how they gather customer feedback and handle complaints.

As a self-service owner, you're going to have to devise ways to stay in touch with your customers, even though you aren't

> **Bright Idea**
>
> If you really want your customers to remember you, why not give out free key chains with punch-out slots that can be used to track your frequent-washer program?

there at all times. One of the ways that many owners accomplish this is to place phone numbers (perhaps your cell phone number) in a conspicuous area of their wash so that customers will always have someone to contact in the event of a problem. If you don't have an office and don't want customers calling you at home, you should install a business line in your home

> **Bright Idea**
>
> If you have a waiting room, offer free coffee or tea to your customers. It doesn't cost you much, and it shows you're doing everything you can to make their experience a pleasant one.

so that customers can leave messages if you don't happen to be available. You can also have your e-mail address posted and check your e-mails regularly. People will contact you from their laptops or Blackberries.

Regardless of the type of wash you operate, when you do get a complaint, it's vitally important that you respond right away. Nothing is more frustrating for a customer than to feel that his or her complaint is falling on deaf ears. If someone calls you and says your equipment malfunctioned and that your machine ate their money, send a refund promptly. Some owners go even further and refund the money lost plus provide a token for a free wash on top of it. What you actually decide to do isn't as important as just making sure that you do something promptly to satisfy the customer.

Measuring Your Success

One of the key components of any marketing plan is that you must know how well it performs for you. If you don't measure the results of your advertising efforts, how will you know if you're spending your money wisely?

Let's take a look at one example of how you might determine what's working and what's not with one of the techniques we've mentioned already—distributing fliers door-to-door. Let's say that on the day you're handing out the fliers, you would expect 50 cars to order a full-service wash, if you did no additional advertising. Let's also assume that you pay one of your employees $8 an hour to distribute the fliers for you, and that each flier has a $2 off coupon attached for a full-service wash. Finally, let's put the price of your full-service treatment at $10 (without any coupons).

Without distributing the fliers, you would be making $500 (50 cars x $10 a car). Now, let's say that your employee works for three hours distributing the fliers, meaning you're incurring $24 in labor costs. You would need only three cars to come in because of the fliers ($8 discounted wash x 3 cars = $24) to make the effort pay for itself. Anything above that, and you're making more money than you would have if you did nothing at all.

To take it one step further, if you are using database marketing to track your customers, you'd be able to determine who among the people who came in that day had

Measuring Your Marketing Efforts

Here's a chart that can help you track the effectiveness of the various market-ing methods you try. When you see how each performs, you can start to make decisions about which are most effective and which you should drop. The meth-ods listed here are just a few examples. You can create your own chart with additional methods as you try them.

Method	Direct Mail	Newspaper Ads	Fliers	Cross-Merchandising	Discount Coupons
Number of new customers					
Total Revenue	$	$	$	$	$
Revenue from each customer (*total revenue divided by number of customers*)	$	$	$	$	$
Total Cost of Campaign	$	$	$	$	$
Cost for each customer (*total cost divided by number of customers*)	$	$	$	$	$
Profit or Loss	$	$	$	$	$

never been to your wash before. As you track them over time, you'll probably find that at least some of them will become regulars. This is when you can truly start to see if the extra effort is worthwhile.

It can be much the same with any other type of marketing effort. The key is to oper-ate your promotion in such a way that you can achieve some sort of measurable result—good or bad. Over time, you'll learn what works best, and what is best left out, of your marketing effort. Like Mike G., the car wash owner in Carson, California, who found, after running lots of different promotional programs, that advertising on the back of supermarket register tapes gave him the most bang for his buck, you'll want to keep track of the estimated gains in business and compare those to the costs it took to achieve those gains. We've provided a chart above to help you track your progress.

Long-Term
Considerations

As your business grows, there are going to be a number of decisions you're eventually going to have to make that will determine the future direction of your car wash. As Yogi Berra once advised, "When you come to a fork in the road, you're going to have to take it." Here are some of the decisions you may find yourself faced with as you grow your business.

▲

Expansion into Other Services or Products

If your business is successful, your customer base will increase and you will begin to develop a solid reputation in the community. At this point, you may start thinking about trying to duplicate the success you've had washing cars and want to expand into other services or products. This is a common practice among car wash owners.

One of the hot trends today is to add quick lube or oil change services. Detailing is another service some owners choose. Whether or not these are right for you really depends on several factors including:

- How much available space you have
- Whether or not you can afford to take on more employees
- The time and costs involved

Assuming there's a need for the services you're thinking about offering and that you can provide what customers want, you're going to be adding another profit center to your business. Therefore, you need to stop and weigh the possibility of extra money against the factors listed above.

Space is often at a premium, so you need to consider carefully what it would take to have cars on the lot for detailing or lube jobs. Would it interfere with your primary business of washing cars? Would it cause logistical problems or do you have a portion of your property available for such a purpose? Could you afford to expand your space, and if so, is there available land adjacent to yours that you could purchase or lease?

New employees mean higher labor costs. Is the demand for such additional services great enough to offset the employee salaries? Can you find good people to handle such jobs as detailing? You may have people already employed who could move to the new positions. Consider these factors and punch the numbers before taking on new profit centers that require additional labor.

The time and costs involved in adding a profit center need to be as minimal as possible. If you are going to have to practically shut down for a week to open a new profit center, you are costing yourself a lot of business. You also need to consider the costs of new equipment and the time it takes to install—and don't forget to inquire as to whether or not your insurance rates will go up. The best plan is one that can be enacted quickly while not disturbing the wash or costing you great sums of money that will take a long time to recoup.

Expansion means learning the ins and outs of a whole new business (new suppliers to find and evaluate, new equipment to learn about, etc.). If you're considering expanding into other areas, it might make sense to start slowly at first. You can always beef up the operation if it turns out to be something you enjoy doing and adds to your bottom line.

In addition to adding offline services—such as quickie lube jobs or oil changes—there's also the possibility that you may want to try to expand your existing business by offering a larger range of wash options. There are any number of different ways in which you can expand. You might convert an existing self-service bay to handle an in-bay automatic unit. Or you may decide to offer the cheaper alternative of an express exterior-conveyor wash at your full-service car wash. There are other options of course, but these are some common ones.

This is probably a somewhat easier task to accomplish than expanding your business into an area with which you're unfamiliar (such as a convenience store). There are definitely some issues to consider if you want to expand into offering products, as opposed to services—as in the case of opening such a store on your property. Remember, one of the things that may have initially attracted you to a car wash business is that you essentially don't have much inventory to worry about. It's the exact opposite with a convenience store. Your entire business is your inventory. Think about whether you want to devote the time to handle this. If not, you may want to think twice about the viability of the project. You can also look into hiring a full-time manager who would handle only that part of the business.

The basic thing you'll want to consider, as you decide whether to branch out into additional services or products, is whether your local market can support what you want to offer. You'll need to conduct market research, just as you did when you initially bought or built your car wash. If you can demonstrate to yourself that the area can support the new business, you've passed the first test.

When you expand into other services, you're once again going to have to go through the process of drawing new customers to your wash. It's likely your efforts won't have to be as involved as with an entirely new business, but it's going to have to be done just the same. Exactly how much work you're going to have to put into this is going to vary. It will tend to be less if you're offering slight upgrades or downgrades in service—adding an in-bay automatic to an existing self-service wash, for example—and a bit more work if the offerings attract radically different segments of the car wash-buying public.

With that said, expanding into other products and services is still a pretty common practice among established car wash owners. It's an option that you'll probably at least consider at some point down the road.

Opening Satellite Locations

This is where you get to become a car wash mogul. Your initial business has done so well that you can imagine a satellite location basically doubling your revenue. This may very well be the case. The biggest difference, however, is that you'll be locked into

becoming an absentee owner at one of your locations, at least part of the time. Because of this, you're going to need an experienced manager who can handle your duties when you're not around. You're probably going to want that manager to oversee operations at your first wash while you concentrate on the new location.

Depending on how much responsibility you turn over to someone else, keep in mind that running two car washes is twice the work of running one car wash. If you're pushing yourself to the limit in terms of time or energy with your first wash, it doesn't make much sense to think that things will get better by adding even more work. However, if you are able to turn over a large portion of the day-to-day duties to a manager, it might be possible to make things work with only a marginal increase in the effort you have to expend.

Most conveyor car wash owners do not own more than one, or perhaps two, washes. As mentioned earlier in the book, the biggest car wash chain in the country has just over 70 locations and there are only a few that have more than a dozen. Typically these chains are centered in one geographic region. This is because of the regional differences and demographics that make it hard to set up one type of wash in numerous places. If you expand to a second or third wash, you should look to expand into areas that are in the same market or in a similar demographic region so that you will have a better idea of what your customers will expect. While getting financial backing is likely to be easier for a second wash if your first one is successful, don't assume that you can duplicate your success without doing similar research to that which you did when you first started planning for your existing car wash.

Valuing and Selling Your Business

There may come a time when you decide it's time to cash out. After years of building your business, you may start thinking about selling it. When you start the selling process, obviously the first thing you're going to want to do is to figure out how much your business is worth. A good place to start is with an appraiser—someone who will look at your facilities and your books and determine what your wash is worth. Local banks and lenders who regularly make loans to the business community will probably have someone who can pass sound judgment. However, it's best to find someone who has experience with in the car wash industry. Don't stop with just one either. Try to get a few opinions so that you can use the higher number as a basis for your negotiations with potential buyers. Also, look online at what car washes are selling for in regions of the country that are similar to yours.

Some other pieces of information that will help you determine a possible selling price are your gross income multiplier (GIM) and net income multiplier (NIM) for similar washes in your area that have sold recently. To figure GIM, divide the selling price of a wash by yearly gross revenue. For example, if a wash sold for $500,000, and it took in $200,000 in revenue, the GIM would be 2.5. The NIM calculation works the same way, just substituting net income for gross revenue. An appraiser can help you with this and then compare these figures with your own. This will help give you an idea of how your wash fits into the overall car wash market in your area.

Stat Fact

More than 55 percent of full-service owners (and 51 percent of exterior-conveyor owners) have been approached about selling their businesses, according to a survey in *Professional Carwashing & Detailing* magazine.

The eventual selling price will be some multiple of the profits you make every year. Exactly what that multiple will be depends on a number of things, including your sales growth rate, the age of your facilities, as well as the GIM and NIM of similar washes in your area.

The timing of your sale is also very important. If you're trying to sell during a period of relatively high interest rates, it's going to be harder for someone to meet the price you're asking. Conversely, during periods of low interest rates, it will be easier for smaller investors to meet their loan payment while still taking a decent profit out of the business. If you find that the times simply aren't conducive to selling your business, it's probably a good idea to wait a while until the economy becomes more favorable.

There are car wash brokers, and you should consider meeting with some to see what they can do to help you sell your car wash.. Take a look at www.carwashbrokers.com, and you'll generally see washes selling for anywhere from $350,000 to $2.7 million, depending on the region in which they are located and the volume of business they handle.

What You Need to Succeed

In the long run, your chances for success in the car wash business will depend on a number of factors—some within your control and a few you can't do anything about. In this section, we'll try to give you some idea of the factors you can control so that you'll be able to maximize your chances for success.

Location, Location, Location

How many times has this topic come up in this guide? Probably more than any other. There's a reason for that. Just about everyone you talk to in the car wash business says location is the number-one factor that will ultimately determine your success or failure. Remember the line from car wash consultant Steve Gaudreau, "I've seen bad car washes in good locations succeed, and good car washes in bad locations fail."

Remember to consider not just traffic count, but site visibility, traffic patterns, street position, local government cooperation (or lack thereof), proximity to competitors, access to labor, signage and zoning regulations, and potential for expansion. These are all important factors that should play a role in how you decide if a location is viable for your car wash.

Service and Quality

Beyond your location, the other factors that will make or break your business all have to do with how you compete with other car washes in your area. The level of service and quality you provide will be paramount. Remember how we told you that car washes can be a fairly homogenous service? That's true to the extent that people will hardly ever drive very far out of their way to get a better wash, if there's another one that does almost as good a job right down the street.

Nevertheless, you shouldn't assume that just because your area is devoid of a competitor that you can let your service and quality slide. For one thing, poor service and quality mean that your regular customers (and they'll only be regulars because you're the only game in town) will probably visit you less often. If it's bad enough, they may drive those extra couple of miles to your nearest competitor or go back to washing the car in their driveway. Remember, your competition is also the home car washer.

Know When to Hold 'Em

In the long run, being able to attract and retain quality employees will be vital to your success, just as it was for Dick H., the car wash entrepreneur in Sacramento, California. "You can't just manage the money," he says. "You need to have competent people running your wash, and you need to pay them well, especially your manager. This is a tough business, and everyone—your employees, your managers, and your customers—are all part of the components that go into running a successful business."

Mike G., the car wash owner in Carson, California, agrees. Even though he has an MBA and has no problem with balance sheets and cash flow analysis, it's still his employees who keep his business humming. "My service writer is probably the most important person I've got," he says. And that's probably the reason his service writer makes more money than anyone else at his wash.

The bottom line is that if you get a reputation for poor service, you're inviting trouble. Word gets around. Your neighbors talk to each other. They know the good businesses in town and the bad ones. Being one of the good ones can only help your cause.

Price

If you have a great location and impeccable service, you can probably get away with charging a bit more than the average for a wash. There's no better example of this than the old competition between the "free with fill up" washes at gas stations and the car wash-only business that charges $5, $10, or more for what appears to be the same service.

Owners who compete with these types of washes say the overriding fear many car wash owners feel when one of these systems goes up near them is unfounded. Sure, some people may take advantage of the free wash once. But after they see what a generally poor job these washes do, they'll be back to you for a real car wash, even though they have to pay more for it.

Mechanical Skill

We've been saying throughout this book that running a car wash is not a job for a desk jockey. Yes, there's some paperwork involved (perhaps quite a bit depending on what type of wash you have), but if it's a cushy office chair you're looking for, you're better off becoming an accountant.

Your business relies on a long list of equipment to run smoothly. And as we all know, anything with moving parts is going to break down sooner or later. When it does break down, your ability to get it up and running again—and quickly—is going to mean the difference between staying in business and shutting down temporarily.

We're not talking about major malfunctions here. Those are most likely going to be handled by the person who sold you the equipment. Rather, we're talking about the minor glitches that can occur on any given day—a malfunctioning weep system that causes your wands to freeze in extremely cold weather, a jammed change machine, a cracked nozzle. If you're someone who can't fathom the thought of changing the oil in your car or fixing a broken pipe, you're going to have a difficult time in the car wash business, unless you have someone on-call 24 hours a day to do these kinds of things for you. And even that's not as reliable an option as being able to do some repairs yourself. Again, consider some courses on repairs and maintenance at a place like the Car Wash College in Florida.

Business Acumen

This is the other side of the coin. With any business, not just a car wash business, your ability to work with numbers, develop a business plan and market it effectively, compete with other businesses, and generally run the show like a professional is going to be one of the factors that determines your success or failure.

So what do you need to know? Well, we're certainly not going to tell you that you have to go back to school and get an MBA. But it does help if you have some general knowledge of how to make, and stick to, a budget, calculate cash flow and revenue projections, determine your level of profitability and return on investment, and just generally make sense of all the numbers you're going to deal with every day.

Unless you pay cash for your wash, you will be paying back lenders or investors. Paying back loans will inevitably come before other things you may want to do—like adding an automatic bay to a self-service wash. If you had plans to expand or modernize when you bought an existing wash, you'll need to be able to assess whether it's practical to do so. Will you still be able to meet your financial obligations to lenders?

You're going to need to be able to determine where your greatest revenue-generating areas are and how to maximize the revenue you get from each car. You should also be able to identify where you may be losing money, and either cut costs or increase revenues to make that area profitable (or eliminate it from your services altogether). If you aren't good at keeping and analyzing records, it will be that much harder for you to operate your business at its maximum potential.

It may be in your best interest to take some evening classes at a local college in finance and money management before you launch your car wash. You will need to have these skills, be ready to make important financial decisions, and act upon them, whenever it is necessary. The owner who can't decide when to end a profitless profit center or cut back on costs if necessary will not last long in this business, and it's an expensive business to get into. Therefore, because the investment is typically a big one for conveyor washes, know about dealing with finances as well as with customers, buying supplies, and working with vendors in advance.

Reliable Suppliers

Time and time again we hear the same thing from car wash owners: "It's the suppliers fault," or to be more exact, the fault of the distributors. Many first-time car wash owners are overly concerned with the type of equipment they buy and the manufacturer who makes it, instead of focusing on the people who can really help you grow your business—local distributors. Remember, equipment needs to be maintained or it may become useless, putting you out of business.

The choice of distributors that you make at the outset of your business, as well as how well you keep up your relationship with your distributors over the course of time, is going to play a large factor in your success. What you're looking for are distributors with a great record of service. You can ask other owners in your area (unless they're a direct competitor of yours, you'll probably get an honest answer) who the top-notch distributors are and then work to build the best relationship you possibly can with them. Again, look for regional car wash associations, such as the Southwest Car Wash Association (www.swcarwash.org) or the Connecticut Car Wash Association (www.wewashctcars.com)—most regions or states have them. Also discuss local distributors with the manufacturers and do research through the International Car Wash Association, the car wash trade magazines, and newspapers such as the two mentioned often throughout this book, *Auto Laundry News* and *Professional Carwashing & Detailing* magazine.

Dedicated Employees

Unless you have a single-bay, self-service wash, you're going to need employees to help you run your car wash. We can't stress enough how the quality of those employees is going to affect your bottom line. While you can think of yourself as the commander of your wash, you're going to need quality front-line troops to be successful.

Over the long term, the kind of employees you have will depend on how successful you are at developing your personnel strategy. How well can you integrate your training program with the overall philosophy of your wash? How well can you manage to retain the top employees you have and get rid of those who don't measure up? How will you compensate your employees to keep them from leaving for greener pastures elsewhere, and how will you replace the ones who do leave?

Ask around and most car wash owners will tell you that a good employee is a tremendously valuable asset. They'll pay them what they have to, and maybe even a little bit more, in order not to lose them. You would be smart to think long and hard about how you plan to make your employees one of your wash's best assets.

Keep Them Coming Back

You'd expect happy customers to return to your car wash, and most likely they will. But no matter how hard you try, there are going to be customers that aren't completely satisfied with the service they receive. How do you turn them around? What's the secret to bringing even dissatisfied customers back to your wash?

The key is not to treat customer complaints as a battle—as a struggle to prove who's right and who's wrong. Instead, if you treat it as a joint effort to find the source of the problem and then to solve it, you'll have a much better chance at winning over all but the most unyielding customers. Steve Gaudreau says that it's possible to get as many as 70 percent of your initially dissatisfied customers back, if you handle the situation properly.

▲

Repeat Customers

Keeping customer returning is very important to the success of your business. As mentioned earlier, it is very costly to keep attracting new customers. Mike G., the car wash owner from Carson, California, has been in the business for six years and never runs advertising. Yet he has a steady flow of cars into his wash every day because he's been able to build a base of customers who know and trust his work. When he first bought his

---

Beyond Your Control

Your success in the car wash business will depend on a number of factors. Some of these will be things you can control, and some will be largely beyond your control. What factors are likely to be out of your control? Take a look at the ones we've listed below.

○ *The weather.* You should take into account as you do your business plan the average number of rainy or snowy days you can expect in the region of the country where you will be opening your business. While global warming and the unpredictability of good old Mother Nature may alter the numbers, you can at least plan in accordance with past weather patterns.

○ *New competition.* If a gas station wants to install an automatic rollover across the street from your wash, there's not much you can do about it. Nor can you do much about the full-service wash down the street installing self-service bays to compete with your own. The best you can do is to open your wash, or buy an existing wash, in an area that is underserved by car washes. If your car wash is an extremely successful business and well established in the neighborhood, it might dissuade others from competing against you. Being very good at what you do makes competition less likely to challenge your success. However, if a new car wash emerges, you can always look for the competitive edge and offer something that the new kid on the block is not offering—remember, you already know the area and the customers.

○ *The economy.* Self-service washes seem to suffer in a poor economy, as do exterior-conveyor and full-service washes, and just about every other type of business. If you're unlucky enough to start your business at the outset of, say, a recession, it might be difficult to turn any kind of meaningful profit until the economy picks up again. In such a situation, you will want to keep your costs as low as possible and perhaps go with an express exterior-only wash for consumers who are watching their money.

---

business, he did advertise. But because he was able to retain those initial customers, he no longer has to expend advertising dollars to draw new ones. If you've created a strong presence in the community and people associate your car wash with quality service, word will get around. The real key to success is keeping your customers satisfied. To do so may require changing with the times or even bucking "the hottest trends" if the clientele likes the way you have been doing business. You need to get a feel for what it is that draws your customers to your wash.

Beyond Your Control, continued

○ *New regulations.* What was once a car wash-friendly business environment could turn decidedly sour overnight with unexpected regulation changes. Talking to zoning boards in your area can be helpful in order to get a feel for what the regulatory environment is likely to be like later on down the road. Stay involved, and aware, of the political climate in your community. Know what is going on that could affect your business. It can't hurt to keep your eyes and ears open for rumblings that could signify new environmental requirements or zoning changes. Be ready to do some lobbying with your local officials in the event of a regulation change that will be particularly costly to your business.

○ *Utility rate increases.* Utilities are going to be a major expense for any car wash owner, and there's very little you can do about it. Besides making sure your equipment is energy efficient, you may need to raise prices to cover the higher utility costs or do a faster wash to save money, while hyping "the quickest wash in town." Always look for a positive slant to a negative situation. Also, provide excellent customer service and be accessible to your regular customers, which doesn't cost you anything.

○ *Water shortages.* When areas of the country experience drought conditions, some of the first businesses affected are usually car washes. Unfortunately, the perception is that car washes are terrible water-wasters. As we've pointed out, this simply isn't true. Other than educating those in charge by providing them with the actual statistics that show how water-friendly car washes are, there's really nothing you can do if your locality decides to shut you down for a period of time. As you might imagine, this can be devastating. If you do happen to find yourself in this situation, you had better hope you have enough cash put away to ride it out. You can also apply, in advance, for business interruption insurance, which covers a business when the ability to function is interrupted by something out of their control.

This doesn't mean that after five years in the business you're going to be seeing the same cars over and over again. You'll get new customers, and with any luck those will become regulars. It also doesn't mean that you'll never want to expand and attract a larger client base, but the core of your business, like most businesses, is most likely going to come from repeat customers.

Tales from the Trenches

We're going to share some of the experiences of the entrepreneurs interviewed for this book so that you can benefit from their hard-won wisdom and guard against the unforeseen pitfalls that strike just about any business from time to time.

Richard K., owner of a ten-bay self-service/in-bay automatic combo outside of Chicago, advises equipping your wash to give yourself a chance to expand your business later on. He says one of the big mistakes he made was not building a pump room large enough to handle the increased water requirements of a number of automatics. It may cost a bit more in the beginning, but it can increase the value of your wash, plus give you more options down the road.

Dick H., the full-service owner in Sacramento, California, who's been in the business since 1975, stresses getting some car wash industry experience—before you buy. He sold car wash products for five years before he bought his own shop. Dick says, "It gave me a lot better feel for the business because we had to pick out and evaluate sites."

According to Mike G., you don't necessarily have to increase the number of customers you serve to be successful. Mike says his volume is actually down 10 percent from the previous owner, but that total sales are up. Why? He changed some procedures (by adding more extensive wash packages) that slowed down the line but increased the average revenue he makes from each car.

If you're going to succeed in the long run, you need to keep on top of changes or new services that your customers are looking for. That's one reason they can be some of your best sources of new ideas for how to improve your wash. Dick H. says he routinely gets new ideas by talking to his customers, including the realization that the time they were willing to wait for service had shrunk dramatically in recent years. If he hadn't gotten that feedback from his customers, he almost certainly would have lost business.

No matter how thoroughly you plan your new business, there are going to be surprises. If you painted too rosy a picture for yourself during the planning phase, these surprises can come back to haunt you later on and could jeopardize your chances for long-term success. For example, Mike G. said he was very surprised that the improvements he planned to make upon buying his site took a lot longer to finish than he initially thought. Luckily, it didn't affect his income. But if you were in the same situation and you were counting on those improvements to increase your customer base and drive up revenue, you might find yourself in a disastrous situation.

The Bottom Line

We began this book by trying to dispel some of the myths you probably believed about the car wash business, and now might be a good time to go back and reiterate one of the more important points. This is not a business that you can run on autopilot. That should be obvious after having gone through all of the material in this guide. You can't simply put down your money, walk away, and watch the profits roll in. But what should also be obvious is that for as long as people drive cars, they're going to need to get them washed. If you can provide that service with a level of quality, for a fair price, and in a reasonable amount of time, you'll be well on the way to success. And on a final note, make sure you take the time to research your chosen industry and properly equip yourself with the tools you'll need to make your new car wash a success. Good luck!

Appendix
Car Wash Resources

They say you can never be rich enough or young enough. While these could be argued, we believe you can never have enough resources. Therefore, we present for your consideration a wealth of sources for you to check into, check out, and harness for your own personal information blitz.

These sources are by no means the only sources out there, and they should not be taken as the Ultimate Answer. We have done our research, but businesses do tend to move, change, fold, and expand. As we have repeatedly stressed, do your homework. Get out and start investigating.

As an additional tidbit to get you going, we strongly suggest the following: If you haven't yet joined the internet Age, do it! Surfing the Net is like waltzing through a vast library, with a breathtaking array of resources literally at your fingertips.

Associations

Some of the regional associations can point you to more local associations and provide current info because there are frequent changes in local contact and membership information. For example, the New York, New Jersey, and Connecticut car wash associations are all now run by the Media Solutions Management Group.

▲

Canadian Carwash Association, (416) 239-0339, Fax: (416) 239-1076, e-mail: office@canadiancarwash.ca, www.canadiancarwash.ca

Car Wash Operators of New Jersey Inc. (CWONJ), 2214 Budd Terrace, Niskayuna, NY 12309, (518) 280-4767, fax: (518) 280-4767, e-mail: mediasolutions@nycap.rr.com, www.cwonj.com

Carwash Association of Pennsylvania, 430 Franklin Church Rd., Dillsburg, PA 17019, (717) 502-1909, fax: (717) 502-1529, e-mail: dwkeefer@adelphia.net, www.pacarwash.org

Chicagoland Carwash Association, P.O. Box 298, Lockport, IL 60441, (708) 301-3568, www.chicagocarwash.org.

Connecticut Carwash Association, 2214 Budd Terrace, Niskayuna, NY 12309, (518) 877-6779, fax: (518) 280-4767, e-mail: mediasolutions@nycap.rr.com, www.wewashcars.com

Heartland Carwash Association, Iowa Membership Area, P.O. Box 932, Des Moines, IA 50304, (515) 965-3190, fax: (515) 965-3191, e-mail: info@heartlandcarwash.org, www.heartlandcarwash.org

International Carwash Association, 401 N. Michigan Ave., Chicago, IL 60611-4267, (312) 321-5199, fax: (312) 245-1085, e-mail: ica@sba.com, www.carwash.org

Mid-Atlantic Car Wash Association, 550M Ritchie Highway, #271, Severna Park, MD 21146, (888) 378-9209 or (410) 647-5780, fax: (410) 544-4640, e-mail: infor@mcacarwash.org, www.mcacarwash.org

Midwest Carwash Association, 3225 W. St. Joseph St., Lansing, MI 48917, (517) 327-9207 or (800) 546-9222, fax: (517) 321-0495, e-mail: info@midwestcarwash.com, www.midwestcarwash.com

New England Carwash Association, 591 North Avenue, Suite. 3-2, Wakefield, MA 01880, (781)245-7400, fax: (781)245-6487, e-mail: neca.org@verizon.net, www.newenglandcarwash.org

New York State Car Wash Association, 2214 Budd Terrace, Niskayuna, NY 12309, (518) 280-4767, fax: (518) 280-4767, e-mail: mediasolutions@nycap.rr.com, www.nyscwa.com

Ohio Car Wash Association, P.O. Box 9113, Canton, OH 44711, (303) 492-8761, e-mail: ocwa1900@aol.com, www.ohiocarwash.com

St. Louis Carwash Association, Country Club Car Wash, 1700 Ford Lane, Saint Charles, MO 63303, (314) 949-5000, fax: (314) 949-5008

Southeastern Carwash Association, 184 Business Park Drive, Suite 200-S, Virginia Beach, VA 23462, (800) 834-9706, fax: (757) 473-9897, e-mail: secwa@secwa.com, www.secwa.com

Southwest Car Association, 4600 Spicewood Springs Rd., #103, Austin, TX 78759, (512) 349-9023 or (800) 440-0644, fax: (512) 343-1530, e-mail: info@swcarwash.org, www.swcarwash.org

Western Carwash Association, 10535 Paramount Blvd., #100, Downey, CA 90241, (562) 928-6928, fax: (562) 928-9557, e-mail: wcarwa@aol.com, www.wcwa.org

Consultants

Car Wash Consultants Inc., P.O. Box 10374, Cedar Rapids, IA 52410-0374, (800) 721-2924 or (319) 294-8307, fax: (319) 294-1686, e-mail: info@carwashconsultantsinc.com, www.carwashconsultantsinc.com

Steve Gaudreau, 275 Elliott St., Beverly, MA 01915, (978) 578-7458, e-mail: steve.gaudreau@hotmail.com

Harvey Miller, 79-498 Cetrino, La Quinta, CA 92253, (760) 771-4149, fax: (760) 771-4768, e-mail: harv@harvsconsulting.com, www.harvsconsulting.com

Steve M. Okun, S. M. Okun & Associates, P.O. Box 3964, Jupiter, FL 33469, (561) 744-6586, e-mail: Steve@SMOKUN.com, www.SMOKUN.com

ProWash Consulting, 9595 Wilshire Blvd., Suite 501, Beverly Hills, CA 90212, (310) 877-2759, fax: (310) 828-2910, e-mail: prowash@prowashconsulting.com, www.prowashconsulting.com

Buying A Car Wash: Brokers & Advisors

Car Wash Advisors - Ameristar Commercial, 7800 Preston, Suite #132, Plano TX, 75024, (972) 618-1047, fax: (972) 421-1715, www.yourcarwashbroker.com

Car Wash Brokers Inc., 10930 N. Tatum Blvd., Suite 106, Phoenix, AZ 85028, (602) 787-1100, fax: (602) 787-1156, www.carwashbrokers.com

Joseph Biello Company LLC, 349 Larkfield Rd., E. Northport, NY 11731, (631) 266-2111, fax: (631) 368-3293, e-mail: carwashsales@josephbielloco.com, www.josephbielloco.com

Helpful Government Agencies

Internal Revenue Service, 1111 Constitution Ave. NW, Washington, DC 20224, (800) 829-1040 or (202) 622-5000, www.irs.gov

Small Business Administration, Answer Desk, P.O. Box 34500, Washington, DC 34500, (800) 827-5722, e-mail: answerdesk@sba.gov, www.sba.gov

U.S. Census Bureau, Washington, DC 20233, (301) 457-4608, www.census.gov

U.S. Department of Labor, Frances Perkins Building, 200 Constitution Ave. NW, Washington, DC 20210, (866) 4-USA-DOL, www.dol.gov

Insurance

Independent Insurance Agents of America, 127 S. Peyton St., Alexandria, VA 22314, (703) 683-4422, www.iiaa.org

The Insurancenter, a company that specializes in insuring car washes, 2901 Arizona Ave., Joplin, MO 64802, (800) 444-8675, fax: (417) 626-2923, www.carwashinsurance.com

National Association of Professional Insurance Agents, 400 N. Washington St., Alexandria, VA 22314, (703) 835-9340, www.pianet.com

Manufacturers and Suppliers

A-OK Equipment & Supply Company, 6031 Pillsbury Ave. So., Minneapolis, MN 55419, (612) 866-2555 or (800) 328-3783, www.aokequipment.com

AIR-serv Group LLC, 1370 Mendota Heights Rd., Mendota Heights, MN 55120, (651) 454-0465 or (800) 247-8363, fax: (651) 454-9542, www.air-serv.com

Autec Car Wash Systems, 2500 W. Front St., Statesville, NC 28687, (800)438-3028 or 704-871-9141, fax: 704-871-9101, pcd@autec-carwash.com, www.autec-carwash.com

Banner Engineering Corp., 9714 Tenth Ave. N., Minneapolis, MN 55441, (763) 544-3164 or (888) 373-6767, fax: (763) 544-3213, e-mail: sensors@bannerengineering.com, www.bannerengineering.com

Blendco Systems LLC, 1 Pearl Buck Court, Bristol, PA 19007, (215)781-3600 or (800) 446-2091, fax: 215-781-3601, e-mail: blendo@blendo.com, www.blendo.com

C.A.R. Products Inc., 630 Beaulieu St., Holyoke, MA 01040-5439, (800) 537-7797, fax: (413) 536-9979, e-mail: carproducts@carproductsinc.com, www.carproductsinc.com

Car Wash Accessories Inc., 3600 Investment Lane, Suite 102, Riviera Beach, FL 33404, (561) 842-0002 or (866) 927-4222, e-mail: info@carwashacc.com, www.carwashass.com

Carwash Superstore LLC, 3350 Hwy 309, North Byhalia, MS 38611, (877) ONE-WASH (663-9274), fax: (662) 893-4611, e-mail: sales@carwashsuperstar.com, www.carwash superstore.com

CAT PUMPS, Car Wash Pumps & Systems, 1681 94th Lane NE, Minneapolis, MN 55449-4324, (763) 780-5440, fax: (763) 780-2958, www.catpumps.com

CATEC Water Recovery and Ozone Systems, 2361 Whitfield Park Ave., Sarasota, FL 34243, (941) 751-5656 or (888) 536-7100, fax: (941) 758-0815, e-mail: cateccwr@aol.com, www.catec.com

Chief's Mfg & Equipment Co., 4325 Monticello Blvd., Cleveland, OH 44121, (800) 433-7758, fax: (216) 291-4222, e-mail: bcomsolo@aol.com, www.chiefsmfg.com

Con-Serv Water Recovery Systems, 605 West Brannen Rd., Lakeland, FL 33807-6160, (863) 644-6925 or (800) 868-9888, fax: (863) 644-2304, e-mail: jckeller@aol.com, www.com-servwater.com

D&S Car Wash Equipment Co., 4200 Brandi Lane, High Ridge, MO 63049, (636) 677-3442, fax: (636) 677-4105, e-mail: sales@dscarwash.com, www.dscarwash.com

Detail Plus Car Appearance Systems Inc., 11650 NE Marx, Portland, OR 97294, (503) 251-2955 or (800) 284-0123, fax: (503) 251-5975, e-mail: detailplus@detailplus.com, www.detailplus.com

Dultmeier Sales, 13808 Industrial Rd., Omaha, NE 68137, (800) 228-9666, fax: (402) 333-5546, e-mail: dultmeir@dultmeir.com, www.dultmeir.com

Econocraft Worldwide Mfg. Inc., 383 Concord Ave., Bronx, NY 10454, (718) 585-6463 or (800) 344-5154, fax: (718) 585-0788, e-mail: sales@econocraft.com, www. econocraft.com

Hi-Performance Wash Systems Inc., 3901 E. 41st Ave., Denver, CO 80216, (303) 322-2232, fax: (303) 322-3307, e-mail: hpws@aol.com, www.hpws.com

Grant Sales, 1701 Capital Ave., Plano, TX 75074, (972) 424-3531 or (800) 767-3531, fax: (972) 881-9017, www.grantsales.com

JBS Industries, 2550 Henkle Dr., Lebanon, OH 45036, (800) 925-8958, e-mail: jstump@jbindustries.com, www. jbindustries.com

J E Adams Industries Ltd., 1025 63rd Ave., SW, Cedar Rapids, IA 52404, (319) 363-0237 or (800) 553-8861, www.jeadams.com

Jim Coleman Company, 5842 W. 34th St., Houston, TX 77092, (713)-683-9878, e-mail: info@jcolemanco.com, www.jcolemanco.com

Joseph Gartland Inc., Beautiful Toweling, 80 West Browning Rd., Bellmawr, NJ 08031-2243, (856) 931-7100 or (800) 222-0086, e-mail: info@beautifulrags.com, www.beautifultoweling.com

LATIMAT Inc., 1040-1 Martingrove Rd., Etobicoke, ON M9W 4W4, Canada, (416) 740-2597 or (416) 579-5845, e-mail: latimat@ica.net, www.latimat.com

MacNeil Wash Systems Ltd., 90 Welham Rd. Barrie, Ontario L4N 8Y4, Canada, (705) 722-7649 or (800) 361-7797, e-mail: info@macneilwash.com, www.macneilwash.com

Mark VII Equipment Inc., 5981 Tennyson St., Arvada, CO 80003, (303) 423-4910 or (800) 525-8248, e-mail: markvii@ markvii.com, www.markvii.com

National Automotive Chemical, 1000 Highland Ave., Cambridge, OH 43725, (740) 439-4699 or (800) 999-7235, e-mail: tmeinert@nachemical.com, www.nachemical.com

Oasis Car Wash Systems, 1909 E. 12th St., Galena, KS 66739, (800) 892-3537, e-mail: mwade@oasiscarwashsystems.com, www.oasiscarwashsystems.com

Ohio Car Wash Supply, 148 W. Broadway, New Lexington, OH 43764, (740) 605-3420, e-mail: sales@ohiocarwashsupply.com, www.ohiocarwashsupply.com

PDQ Manufacturing Inc., 1698 Scheuring Rd., De Pere, WI 54115, (920) 983-8333 or (800) 227-3373, e-mail: domesticsales@pdqinc.com, www.pdqinc.com

PECO Car Wash Systems, 244 Rex Blvd., Auburn Hills, MI 48326, (248) 299-5800 or (800) 448-3946, e-mail: sales@pecocarwash.com, www.pecocarwash.com

Powerain Systems Inc., One Enterprise Dr., Tower, MN 55790, (800) 943-8866, e-mail: info@powerain.com, www.powerain.com

PurClean Spot-Free Rinse Systems, 3315 Orange Grove Ave., North Highlands, CA 95660, (800) 818-8868, e-mail: lghirsh@purclean.com, www.purclean.com

RYKO Mfg Co., 11600 N.W. 54th Ave., Grimes, IA 50111, (515) 986-3700, e-mail: sales@ryko.com, www.ryko.com

Sonny's: The Car Wash Factory, 5605 Hiatus Rd., Tamarac, FL 33321, (954) 720-4100 or (800) 327-8723, www.sonnysdirect.com

Unitec Electronics, 7125 Troy Hill Drive, Elkridge, MD 21075, (443) 561-1200 or (800) 4UNITEC, www.unitecelectronics.com

Car Wash Training

Car Wash College, 5605 Hiatus Rd., Tamarac, FL 33321, (866) 492-7422, sgaudreau@carwashcollege.com, www.carwashcollege.com

Emplolyee Background Checking Services

Criminal Data at www.criminaldata.com

InfoCublic at www.infocublic.com

Personnel Profiles at www.personnelprofiles.com

Public Record Service at www.publisrecordservice.com

Publications

American Clean Car magazine, 500 N. Dearborn St., Chicago, IL 60610, (312) 337-7700

Auto Laundry News, 2125 Center Ave., #305, Fort Lee, NJ 07024, (201) 592-7007, www.carwashmag.com

Professional Carwashing & Detailing magazine, National Trade Publications, 13 Century Hill Dr., Latham, NY 12110, (518) 783-1281, www.carwash.com

Self-Service Car Wash News magazine, P.O. Box 6341, Grand Rapids, MI 49516, e-mail: jjjsscwn@aol.com

The Carwash Appraisal Handbook, Crowe Enterprises, 600 W. 70th St., Kansas City, MO 64113, e-mail: pcrowe@juno.com

Software

Innovative Control Systems Inc., 1349 Jacobsburg Rd., Wind Gap, PA 18091, (800) 642-9396, e-mail: info@washnet.com, www.washnet.com

Integrated Services Inc. (ISI), 12242 S.W. Garden Place, Portland, OR 97223, (503) 968-8100 or (800) 922-3099, e-mail: isi@ints.com, www.ints.com

DRB Systems Inc., P.O. Box 550, Uniontown, OH 44685, (800) 336-6338, e-mail: info@drbsystems.com, www.drbsystems.com

Sources of Referrals

The American Bar Association, 541 N. Fairbanks Ct., Chicago, IL 60611, (312) 988-5522, www.aba.org

The American Institute of Certified Public Accountants, 1211 Ave. of the Americas, New York, NY 10036, www.aicpa.org

National Association of Insurance and Financial Advisors, 2901 Telestar Ct., P.O. Box 12012, Falls Church, VA 22042, (703) 770-8100, www.naifa.org

National Association of Small Business Accountants, 526 Davis St., #217, Evanston, IL 60201, (866) 296-0001, www.smallbizaccounts.com

The National Council of Architectural Registration Boards, 1801 K St. NW, #1100K, Washington, DC 20006-1310, (202) 783-6500, www.ncarb.org

Web Sites

CarWashConsignment.com, a meeting place for buyers and sellers of car wash equipment, www.carwashconsignment.com

The Carwash Forum, a web site where car wash owners gather to discuss the business, www.carwashforum.com, also known as www.autocareforum.com

Glossary

3 and 1: typical setup for a self-service wash; refers to a wash consisting of three self-service bays and one in-bay automatic unit.

Automatic rollover: see In-bay automatic.

Bay: the physical structure housing self-service or automatic rollover equipment.

Conveyor: a motorized track that pulls a car or truck so that washing machinery cleans the car.

Cycle: a period of time for which a self-service wash operates; usually around four minutes.

Detail: services related to cleaning the interior of an automobile.

Express exterior: a fast, exterior-only wash, popular trend in conveyor washes.

Exterior-conveyor (or exterior-only): a type of wash that uses a conveyor system but does not include any interior cleaning.

FlexServe: a replacement for the traditional full-service car wash format that allows for total service options for car wash operators, giving them flexibility to cater to their marketplace, adjust for weather patterns, cross-train labor, and so on.

Full-service car wash: a type of wash that includes a complete wash of the exterior as well as cleaning of the interior of a vehicle.

Greeter: someone who greets customers and write down, or uses a touchscreen computerized system to take down, what services they want. Greeters (aka service writers) also try to enhance sales.

ICA: International Carwash Association.

In-bay automatic (or automatic rollover): a type of wash consisting of a machine that moves, or rolls over, a stationary vehicle.

Menu of services: the list of services or wash packages a company provides.

Offline services: extra cleaning services (such as vacuuming or carpet/upholstery cleaning) performed that are not part of the standard wash process; also non-wash-related services such as oil change, quickie lube, etc.

Phase I environmental study: a study that can limit your liability for environmental damage by calculating the amount of damage already done to a site by a previous owner.

Reclaim system: a system installed to reclaim, cleanse, and use the same water again, thus creating a more environmentally sound car wash.

Return on investment (ROI): a method of calculating the attractiveness of an investment; ROI is computed by dividing annual profit by the amount of money invested in the enterprise.

Run-off: water that has been used in the wash process.

Self-service car wash: a type of wash where the customer washes the car himself using equipment supplied by the car wash operator.

Stacking space: the area available on your lot where cars can wait for washing equipment to become free.

Start-up: the first cycle for a self-service wash.

Touch-free system (or touchless): a washing system that uses high-pressure water jets, as opposed to a brush-based system, to clean a car's exterior.

Tunnel: the physical structure that houses a conveyor washing system.

Up-sell: the practice of selling additional, or more expensive, goods or services to a customer who initially wants to buy a less expensive product.

Wand: the piece of equipment self-service customers use to dispense and spread water, soap, wax, and other materials over an automobile.

Water hardness: a measure of metal salts present in water; water that is hard (more than five grains) can leave spots on cars when dry.

Weep system: a system designed to prevent freezing in pipes and wands by allowing a slow trickle of water to escape the machinery.

Index

▲